Bonham Ward Bax

The Eastern seas

Being a narrative of the voyage of H. M. S.

Bonham Ward Bax

The Eastern seas
Being a narrative of the voyage of H. M. S.

ISBN/EAN: 9783337173968

Printed in Europe, USA, Canada, Australia, Japan

Cover: Foto ©Andreas Hilbeck / pixelio.de

More available books at **www.hansebooks.com**

THE EASTERN SEAS.

The Revd H Burnside
from Mrs Bonham Bax
in memory of her husband
the Author.
Sept 22nd, 1877

FUSI-YAMA MOUNTAIN, FROM HACONE.

THE EASTERN SEAS:

BEING

A NARRATIVE OF THE VOYAGE OF H.M.S. "DWARF"
IN CHINA, JAPAN, AND FORMOSA.

WITH A

DESCRIPTION OF THE COAST OF RUSSIAN TARTARY AND EASTERN
SIBERIA, FROM THE COREA TO THE RIVER AMUR.

By CAPTAIN B. W. BAX, R.N.

WITH MAP AND ILLUSTRATIONS.

LONDON:
JOHN MURRAY, ALBEMARLE STREET.
1875.

LONDON:
BRADBURY, AGNEW, & CO., PRINTERS, WHITEFRIARS.

PREFACE.

In consequence of H.M.S. "Dwarf" having visited many places in China, Japan and the Russian possessions on the eastern coast of Siberia about which very little has been written up to the present time, I have endeavoured to describe her commission of three years and eight months in those seas and the places visited.

Many people will be interested to know something about the Russian ports in the eastern seas of which at present little is generally known, although so much has been published about Russia in Central Asia.

They will probably be surprised at the large strides made by that power on the sea-coast of Tartary, and the possession of splendid harbours which are capable of holding large fleets and of being made almost impregnable; for instance, such as the harbour of Vladivostok, which is about to become the head-quarters of the naval forces in Eastern Siberia.

Eastern Siberia now includes all the latest annexations in Tartary, the establishment at Nikolaevsk on the river Amur being too far north for a naval station on account of the extreme cold in the winter freezing the river up for several months, and also on account of the shallow bar at the entrance.

The very able work called the "Upper and Lower Amur" by T. W. Atkinson, F.R.G.S., F.G.S., describes the interior possessions of Russia up to 1860; but since that period the Russians have settled themselves firmly on the sea coast close down to the borders of the Corea, which will give them a splendid base of operations for naval warfare in the eastern seas, should the necessity arise.

I have also endeavoured to describe the Japanese troops and vessels that formed their expedition to

Preface.

Formosa, and the cause of it. Although to the casual observer small results were apparently obtained, the real effect has been to compel the Chinese to acknowledge their responsibility for the conduct of the tribes on the east coast of Formosa, towards shipwrecked people. Hitherto they had always replied to complaints of foreign nations, by stating that they had no control over the savage tribes on the east coast, and that the foreigners must punish them themselves. This had been the case when an American vessel had been wrecked, and the crew murdered at the south end of Formosa; the United States had been obliged to send vessels of war to punish the savage tribe, in consequence of the Chinese expressing their inability to do so.

Many people in England will be pleased to hear that the missionaries at several of the ports in China have turned their attention to the spiritual wants of the sailors of their own country as well as to the conversion of the natives; and that there are many good and benevolent gentlemen among the officials and merchants who have given both their time and their money for making respectable places for our seamen to resort to while on leave, where they can read the papers and get their meals quietly and soberly. These efforts have been crowned with a very visible effect in the suppression of drunkenness and leave-breaking in the fleet, and have considerably reduced the great cause of sickness and invaliding from that station; thus rendering a great benefit to the country in general, as well as to the men individually.

The description of some of my journeys inland will afford a slight idea of the manner in which the missionary work is carried on, and of the hardships endured by some of the missionaries in performing their duty.

For the historical references I have consulted the works of Père Gaubil, a Jesuit Father, Dixon on Japan, the Chinese Repository, Captain Basil Hall's voyages, and the voyage of H.M.S. "Blossom," by Captain Beechey, R.N.

CONTENTS.

CHAPTER I.

DEPARTURE FROM ENGLAND, AND PASSAGE OUT IN H.M.S. "TAMAR," APRIL, 1871—ST. VINCENT—ASCENSION—ST. HELENA—THE CAPE—NATAL—MAURITIUS—SINGAPORE—HONGKONG—H.M.S. "DWARF" COMMISSIONED JULY 18TH, 1871—TYPHOON AT HONGKONG—AMOY—SWATOW—TAKOW IN S. FORMOSA—JOURNEY TO BAKSA—TAI-WAN-FOO. . 36

CHAPTER II.

THE HISTORY OF FORMOSA 56

CHAPTER III.

THE NEIGHBOURHOOD OF AMOY—JOURNEY UP THE NORTH RIVER—DRAGGING A SCHOONER OFF THE BEACH IN FORMOSA—VISIT TO THE MISSION STATIONS S. W. OF AMOY—THE FOO-CHOW STATION—KELUNG—SAU-O-BAY—THE LOO-CHOO ISLANDS—TAM-SUI 104

CHAPTER IV.

WRECK OF THE "YEDDO"—MONASTERY ON THE CUSHAN MOUNTAIN—DISTURBANCE AT TWA-TU-TIA IN FORMOSA—VISIT TO THE SAVAGE TRIBES IN THE INTERIOR—FÊTE AT THE ARSENAL AT FOO-CHOW 137

Contents.

CHAPTER V.

SEARCH FOR A LORCHA—CHIN-CHEW—ARRIVE AT JAPAN—ACCOMPANY THE COMMANDER-IN-CHIEF TO KOBÉ AND NAGASAKI 156

CHAPTER VI.

VOYAGE TO THE RUSSIAN POSSESSIONS IN TARTARY AND EASTERN SIBERIA—THE ISLAND OF YESSO 192

CHAPTER VII.

ASCENT OF FUSI-YAMA MOUNTAIN IN JAPAN . . . 216

CHAPTER VIII.

KOBÉ—SHANGHAI—THE HOMES FOR SEAMEN—REBELLION AT SAGA IN JAPAN—SEARCH FOR THE CREW OF A SCHOONER THAT HAD FOUNDERED—KITE-FLYING FESTIVAL . . . 246

CHAPTER IX.

THE JAPANESE EXPEDITION TO FORMOSA—THE ARRIVAL OF THREE CANOES AT KELUNG FROM THE PELLEW ISLANDS—JAPANESE CAMP AT LIANG-KIOU, S. FORMOSA . . 274

CHAPTER X.

NAGASAKI—EFFECTS OF TYPHOON, AUGUST 20TH, 1874—SHANGHAI—CHING-KIANG—NANKING—NINGPO—HONG-KONG—RELIEVED BY THE NEW SHIP'S COMPANY, NOVEMBER 30TH, 1874 287

LIST OF ILLUSTRATIONS.

	PAGE
FUSI-YAMA MOUNTAIN, FROM HACONE	(*Frontispiece*.
BEATING OUT THE RICE	19
PEPPO-HOAN WOMAN AND CHILD, BAKSA	29
"CATAMARAN," FORMOSA	35
THE CAPTURE OF AMOY BY THE MANDARIN FORCES, 1853	57
PUMPING WATER INTO THE RICE FIELDS	61
POTTED ANCESTORS, AMOY	64
SAVAGE MAN AND WOMAN, FORMOSA	124
PAPPENBORG ISLAND, WHERE THE CHRISTIANS WERE THROWN OVER THE CLIFF, A.D. 1636	153
VLADIVOSTOK, EASTERN SIBERIA	160
WEDGE-SHAPED PROCESSION OF GIRLS	163
JAPANESE MOUNTAIN COOLIE	199
JAPANESE JUNK	222

THE EASTERN SEAS.

CHAPTER I.

DEPARTURE FROM ENGLAND, AND PASSAGE OUT IN H.M.S. TAMAR, APRIL, 1871—ST. VINCENT — ASCENSION — ST. HELENA—THE CAPE — NATAL — MAURITIUS — SINGAPORE — HONGKONG —H.M.S. DWARF COMMISSIONED JULY 18TH, 1871—TYPHOON AT HONG-KONG—AMOY—SWATOW—TAKOW IN S. FORMOSA—JOURNEY TO BAKSA—TAI-WAN-FOO.

On Tuesday, the 11th of April, 1871, H.M. troopship "Tamar" left Old England with the ships' companies for the gun-vessels "Dwarf" and "Avon," and also with a detachment of troops for St. Helena, the Cape, Natal, and Mauritius. The "Tamar" was a very comfortable vessel, steaming her 200 miles a day without much consumption of coal, and was a very good sea-boat. We were fortunate in having a pleasant set of officers on board, and soon after getting clear of the Channel had games in the evening on deck, and readings and lectures occasionally in the saloon, as the captain encouraged every sort of rational amusement among the officers and men.

On the 24th we arrived at St. Vincent, Cape Verde Islands, where we coaled. While here, several of us got some good quail shooting about five miles from the town, or rather village. The whole island looks such a parched up cinder, that it is difficult to believe any birds could live on it at all, were there not a little dried grass on the opposite side of the island to the town. The population consists of the negroes engaged at the coal dépôt and a very few white people. As there was generally a strong north-east wind blowing while we were here, we did not feel the heat so much when out shooting, although under a scorching sun, as we expected.

On the 26th of April we left with a strong, fair wind for Ascension, where we arrived on the 5th of May. When about 190 miles from Ascension, we saw great quantities of birds called "wide-awakes." The wide-awakes are sea birds resembling small gulls, but are black on the back and white under the wings and breast. They all live together in a valley at Ascension called "Wide-awake Fair," where they lay their eggs so thickly on the rocks, that it is difficult to walk through the Fair without breaking them. The birds defend their eggs most desperately, and fly around and screech when disturbed. The eggs are very good eating when fresh. Most of us visited the fair, and also the highest peak of the island, which is called "Green Mountain," from a patch of green grass and trees on the top. Ascension is a naval settlement, and when we were there, was under the command of a commander with 130 officers and men, many of whom had their families with them. They all received rations as if they were living on board a man-of-war, as the supplies on the island are limited. There is only one small stream of water from the peak; water has therefore to be condensed occasionally to supply the garrison and any vessel that calls in for it.

There is a hospital at the top of the mountain as as well as one at the foot, near the landing-place; which are principally used by patients from the African squadron.

There are also several small houses on Green Mountain, to which the officers can go for change of air. Cattle and sheep are kept at a farm on the mountain, plenty of turtle are caught in one of the bays, and kept in the turtle ponds till wanted, and the reefs abound with good fish. The landing-place is very bad and inconvenient; you have to watch your opportunity to jump on shore as the boat rises with the wave, and if the rollers set in, which they sometimes do very suddenly, no boats could land for days on account of the heavy surf.

We left Ascension on the 9th of May, and arrived at St. Helena on the 13th, where nearly all got away for a scamper to Longwood. Some parts of St. Helena are pretty; there are a few streams on the island, and one good waterfall.

The formation and soil appear the same sort of cinder as Ascension, but probably of an older formation, as it possesses much more vegetation. The Suez Canal has damaged the commercial prosperity of the town to a great extent, by diverting most of the trade that formerly went round by the Cape to India and China.

We left St. Helena the same evening, and arrived at the anchorage off Cape Town on the 21st, where we landed most of the soldiers, and were sorry to part with them; though they all appeared heartily glad to get on terra firma again. It is a pity that the breakwater at Table Bay is not extended sufficiently to shelter large vessels, because at present it is much exposed in bad weather. After landing our troops we steamed on to the naval station at Symon's Bay, where we found H.M. ships "Sirius" and "Megæra;" the latter of which was on the way to her sad end at St. Paul's Island. There is very good sea-fishing in the bay, and there are partridges and apes a few miles from Symon's Town. The road to Cape Town, near Constantia and Wynberg, is very pretty, from the neat houses, which are surrounded with gardens; the avenues of fir trees along each side of the road make a most grateful shade.

The hotel at Wynberg is clean and reasonable, and much pleasanter to stop at than those in Cape Town.

We proceeded on our voyage on the 2nd of June; and, when outside the bay, well clear of the land, picked up a boat without any one in it. We supposed that it had belonged to a French coolie ship, that had been lost with all hands not long before. On the 6th we anchored off Natal. As there was a heavy surf on the bar, there was some little difficulty in landing the soldiers; however, the next day a flat-bottomed bar boat, built like a cargo boat, took them all in, where they were covered with hatches to keep the water from getting below, and were then safely towed over the bar by a steamer into the river. We then steamed on to Mauritius, where we arrived on the 14th.

Although Mauritius is very pretty and possesses

magnificent mountain scenery, yet I think its beauty has been overrated, on account of there being few large trees on the island; those that it possesses have been painfully twisted about and broken by hurricanes, and also considerably reduced by being cut recklessly for fuel. Altogether the island appeared to have a very used-up appearance. A great difficulty the authorities had to contend with, was the means of getting rid of the coolies when their term of service had expired. The coolies were brought from India, but no provision had been made for their return. The island had therefore accumulated a large worn-out black population, which was a fruitful source of fever, and suffered frightfully from its ravages. The Government had endeavoured, but unfortunately without success, to pass an act to compel the employers to send the coolies back after their term of service had expired, as most of them by that time had managed to save sufficient to live comfortably at home in India, among their friends, but not to pay their passage home as well. The planters were mostly French; there were very few English in the island. The whole population was put down to about 350,000. Fever was very prevalent, some said that the excessive use of guano caused it; but as no effectual measures were taken to keep the water pure by preventing the Hindoos and Chinese from washing their clothes in, and otherwise polluting the streams that supplied the houses with drinking water, it was most probably caused by this also. The botanical gardens are very well laid out, and reflect great credit on the taste of the French governor who planned them. On the 17th we left for Hongkong, where we arrived on the 15th of July, having called at Singapore on our way for coal, and to land a few passengers. At Hongkong we found the "Avon" and "Dwarf" in the harbour, ready to receive the new ships' companies, the term of service of their former ones having expired.

On the afternoon of the 17th of July, 1871, the new ships' companies were sent on board of H.M. ships "Dwarf" and "Avon," the former ones having been discharged in the forenoon, and afterwards sent to England. The pendant was hoisted at 8 A.M. on the 18th.

Hongkong has become nearly double in size and population since I remember what it was in 1853. Many trees have been planted, but the frequency of typhoons keeps them from increasing very fast; and the Chinese are constantly cutting them for firewood, which is scarce and dear at Hongkong. There is a good reservoir for water about four miles from Hongkong. It is formed by a dam made across the end of a valley, which is supplied by a stream from the hills above. In the spring, when the mountains have their green coat on, the island looks very pretty, and the harbour quite alive with the quantity of steamers, vessels, junks, and Chinese boats of all descriptions, that dart about in every direction; many of the boats being managed entirely by Chinese women and their young families, the husband working as a coolie on shore.

On the 3rd of August a telegram was received from Batavia, stating that a boat from H.M. ship "Megæra" had arrived there, with a lieutenant and some of the crew of that ship, bringing the news that the "Megæra" had been beached on St. Paul's Island to prevent her from sinking; and that the ship's company had been safely landed on the island, but required immediate assistance. The Commodore at once chartered the Peninsular and Oriental steamer "Malacca," that happened to be laying in the harbour, and sent her to the rescue, laden with the necessary stores and provisions.

On the 31st the "Dwarf" went outside the harbour to try her engines, having been refitted and reported ready for sea.

After the trial we remained outside for the purpose of exercising the ship's company, firing at a target, and other drills, to get the men into their places as soon as possible. While steaming into a bay to anchor in the evening we passed some large floating fishing stakes, which were moored in twelve fathoms of water. Unfortunately, a bamboo hawser attached to one of them got foul of our port propeller, and as it was very tough and hard, and as thick as a man's wrist, we had much trouble in cutting through it. We were compelled to heel the ship by getting all the guns and shot and other weights over to the opposite side of the deck, so as to raise the propeller as near the surface of the water as possible. An officer, carpenter, and a seaman then dived under the water, and managed to cut through it with axes and saws. The next day the barometer began to fall, and a long swell came up from the S.E. direction; the sky having a dirty, greasy look at the same time, with every indication of a typhoon coming on, we went into harbour. On the 2nd it commenced to blow hard from the N.W., the wind changing gradually to N.E., when it blew the hardest, and the barometer was at its lowest, 29·20 ins., at 11 P.M. After that it continued to change to E., and finished at S.E. in the forenoon; the barometer rising again as the weather moderated. There was a great deal of damage done to ships, junks, and boats; many lives were lost, as several small vessels foundered, and some were blown out to sea and wrecked outside. Nearly every vessel dragged their anchors. Although we had three anchors down and were steaming as well, the lower yards and topmasts being down on deck and everything else sent from aloft, yet we managed to drag our anchors till we got close under the bow of the "Princess Charlotte;" so close, that it appeared as if her great cutwater must strike our stern as she pitched to the waves. Fortunately we had not veered quite all our cable; we therefore watched our opportunity, and gave her full speed with the engines, the helm being placed hard over to port at the same time, and then veered on the cables quickly. The ship answered her helm and sheered clear of the "Princess Charlotte," bringing up safely under her stern. The houses in the town were much damaged, and the sea-wall was washed away by the waves for a considerable distance.

After the typhoon, H.M.S. "Avon" was sent outside the harbour to look out for the wrecks, and to assist any disabled vessels that she might meet with. Shipwrights at Hongkong ought to do well in the typhoon season from the quantity of vessels that come in, having lost their masts or boats, and often badly strained in the hull besides.

For a long time after the typhoon working parties of seamen from the men-of-war were employed in raising the coal-lighters belonging to the naval dockyard. The lighters had been old condemned gunboats, and had foundered in the storm. In order to do this, a gunboat was placed on each side of the one to be lifted, and chains were passed under her bottom and secured to two balks of timber, which were placed across the gunboats near the bow and stern. These chains were hove taut at low water, and as the tide rose the lighter floated, and was then hauled in towards the shore until it again grounded. This operation had to be repeated every tide until it was far enough in to allow of its being pumped out at low water. We had hot, showery weather during the work, which was most trying for the working parties.

On the 11th October we left for Amoy, but in consequence of the strong N.E. monsoon against us obliging us to anchor often, we made a long passage; and in consequence of calling in at Swatow on our way, did not reach Amoy till the 22nd, just as the Commander-in-Chief, Vice-Admiral Sir H. Kellet, K.C.B., was leaving that place in H.M. ship "Ocean," for Hongkong. I was surprised to see what a pretty and pleasant place the foreign settlement had become since the merchants' houses have been built on the island of Kulangsue opposite the town instead of being confined to the town side, as was the case when I was at Amoy in 1853. The old settlement is merely used for offices and business transactions. There is a very pleasant little community consisting of English, American, French, and German; a club and racket court have been built on the island, which has been laid out with walks, quite clear of any intrusion from the Chinese.

We found the merchants very hospitable, and the ladies often gave pleasant croquet parties; in fact everyone seemed to try how agreeably they could make the time pass to others as well as themselves during their exile in a foreign land. Amoy is one of the stations for English and American missionaries, who live on the island of Kulangsue with their families, and take their regular turn of duty up the country. They go as far as the city of Chinchew, which is about eighty miles up the coast, and for a radius of sixty miles or so inland. The Foochow mission stations almost join theirs on the north and the Swatow on the south.

It necessitates constant hard and trying travelling, sometimes by boat on the rivers, and at others on foot, or by chairs carried by coolies, to visit the chapels at those towns and villages where their efforts have been successful in establishing a small Christian community among the Chinese.

Amoy possesses a hospital for the Chinese, which is supported by the foreign merchants, and is very ably attended by an English doctor. Among his patients he has many diseases to contend with that are not common in England. A clergyman visits the hospital every morning, and holds a service for those patients that will attend. There is also a school for children.

At this time a steam gun-boat belonging to the Chinese Imperial Custom service was at Amoy, and engaged in building the lighthouse on Chapel Island about sixteen miles from the harbour. Her captain (who had been in the English navy) kindly asked me to go with him one day to see it, when he had to take provisions and water to the island, which offer I gladly availed myself of. The island is merely an egg-shaped rock about 180 feet high; the lighthouse is 42 feet besides, and it shows a good flashing light for twenty-one miles. As there was no water on the island, they have built two tanks to catch the rain; and also a comfortable house for the keepers, and a store-house to hold a good supply of provisions, as boats can only land at it when the water is smooth. The rock is quite precipitous from the water, and the path to the top is only a narrow ledge scraped out of the side of the cliff; the task of getting the heavy materials, and especially the lantern, to the top, was most difficult, and great credit is due to the ingenuity and perseverance of the engineer and those who were employed with him. A very curious cave runs through the centre of the rock. The water all round the island is very deep, the only place where the gun-boat could drop her anchor for a few hours in fine weather being quite close to the landing place.

There are some nice walks in the vicinity of Amoy to the different Buddhist temples in the hills at the back of the city. One or two old priests live in them, who lead a quiet and peaceful existence, and are supported by small donations from the Chinese, and in some cases by cultivating a small patch of ground belonging to the temple, as well. They are always glad to afford the use of the temples to a picnic party, and consider it no sacrilege to have the good cheer spread on the joss tables for a small consideration. The carving in some of the temples is very quaint, and painted with the most glaring colours; altogether they look very curious, as they are perched among the large granite boulders, and shaded with fine fir trees, which are carefully preserved near the temples, although they are very scarce elsewhere among the bare and scorched-up hills of Amoy.

On the 31st of October, a request came from the master of the British schooner "Rantipole," to have his vessel surveyed, as she had been driven on shore on one of the "Pescadore" islands about eighty miles from Amoy. The vessel had been got off with great difficulty, and came back to Amoy with the assistance of H.M. gunboat "Opossum." The story shows how a good and brave seaman can defend his ship, and save her under very trying circumstances, and with small resources. The schooner had been caught in a very heavy gale when off the "Pescadores," and all her sails had been blown away; at last, as the vessel had become unmanageable, she had been driven over a reef on one of the out-lying islands. After the storm was over, the crew laid out their anchors to heave the vessel off; and as all their boats had been smashed, and they could hire none from the fishermen, who refused to render any assistance, they made rafts, and took their anchors out with them, and by this method managed to haul their vessel into a narrow channel between the reefs, and commenced to warp her out. The Chinese at these islands being

plunderers (when they get a chance), as well as
fishermen, and always looking on a wreck as lawful
spoil, when they saw the schooner likely to get
away, swarmed round her in boats, and tried to get
on board to plunder her. The crew consisting of
eleven Manilla men besides the captain, who was a
big and strong west countryman, behaved very
bravely, and beat the Chinese back. Finding they
could not take the schooner by force, the Chinese
then tried to lift the anchor with their boats, so
that she would drift on the rocks again. On
seeing this the captain fired at them, and drove
them away. On account of a strong N.E. wind
continuing to blow into this little channel, the
schooner could not get away without assistance.
Fortunately a steamer happened to call at Makung,
the principal town on the island, and heard about
the circumstances; and on her return to the China
coast reported it, so that the "Opossum" went
over and towed the schooner out of her dangerous
place, much to the disgust of the fishermen.

On the night of November 1st the steamer
"Azof" broke from her moorings, and before the
crew had time to save her by letting go an anchor,
she drifted on a nasty reef of large boulder rocks
off the seaman's hospital on Kulangsue Island;
nearly on the same rocks that the "Fox" frigate

is represented to have been lost in the seventeenth century, as described in Hamilton's voyages.

Unfortunately the "Azof" grounded when it was near high water, and as the rise and fall of the tide is fully nineteen feet at spring tides, the rocks soon went though her bottom, and she became a total wreck. The "Fox" was the first British King's ship that ever visited Amoy, and Captain Hamilton gives a very interesting account of the manner in which the crew were disposed of, and the great difficulty the East India Company's ships made before they would take the officers and seamen on board their vessels for passage to England, and Captain Hamilton states that it was only on account of the pressure put on them by the Chinese tauti, or governor, who threatened to stop the trade if they did not assist their countrymen, that they at last consented. Chinese governors at that time acted in a far more independent manner towards foreigners than they can now. There are some of the graves of the East India Company's officers who were buried on Kulangsue Island at a very early date, the inscriptions being still legible. On the city side of the harbour there are some belonging to Portuguese Jesuits, buried there at the end of the sixteenth century.

On the 8th of November we ran down to Swatow

under sail, and arrived off the settlement the next day. Swatow is situated on the river Han, the Chinese town being built on a mud flat on the north bank of the river, and the foreign settlement on the other side of it; all of the merchants' offices are in the native town. A range of rugged and rocky hills rises immediately behind the settlement, which is built at the base of them, some of the houses being surrounded with trees, which give a pleasing relief to the eye from the glare of the barren hills above. Swatow is the port for the large city of Tou-chow-foo, which is about twenty-eight miles up a river that is only navigable for small flat-bottomed boats. An English vice-consulate is held at Tou-chow-foo, and the consulate is at Swatow; all the trade is carried on and the foreign vessels anchor at the latter place. Behind the city, in the swamp, are plenty of duck and snipe. The Chinese have very ingenious nets for catching the fish in the lagoons which are staked, and used for breeding.

While at Swatow I took the opportunity to survey a creek called Tatapo, leading from Swatow to Hope Bay on the coast to the south. It cuts off twenty miles, and is a capital passage for boats, as the point called the Cape of Good Hope, where there is always a nasty tide-race, would be avoided.

It is about eight miles long, but very shallow at each entrance, only having about six feet of water at high water; although when once inside the creek there is plenty of water. This passage is much used by junks.

On the 19th of November the captain of the

BEATING OUT THE RICE.

Chinese Imperial gunboat "Chento," and myself, started in his gig, with a crew of six Chinese sailors, to examine the water communication in the neighbourhood. We sailed up the river Han, with a strong fair wind and tide, to the town of Cheek-yuen, about thirty miles from Swatow, in six and a half hours. The country was flat, and highly cultivated with rice, and intersected with canals in every direction. The people were cutting the rice, and stacking it in sheaves like wheat in England. It was afterwards beaten out into big tubs in the fields, when thoroughly dry. We fortunately found a Chinese passenger steamboat at Cheek-yuen, and slept on board of her during the night, as we had only an open boat. The next morning we walked round the city walls, which were about three miles in circuit. The houses were mean, and many of them in ruins. After breakfast we started in our boat through narrow canals and creeks among the paddy-fields to a village called Torkar, about twenty miles from Cheek-yuen. We here left the boat, and walked on to the city of Tou-chow-foo, which was about thirteen miles farther. The paths across the fields were very narrow, barely sufficient for two people to pass each other. They generally consist of a series of stones placed lengthwise, about the width of a respectable curb-stone. The country people were all very civil. On approaching the city, our path led through orange groves, and we met many Chinese gentle-men out for a stroll on foot and horseback, enjoy-ing the shade of the trees. As neither of us spoke Chinese, we had a difficulty in finding our way to the consulate, the city being very large and bustling. It has a high wall round it in a good state of preservation. In one place a play was being acted on a stage raised about five feet from the ground, and stretching right across the street. The crowd in front of it was so dense, that we had much trouble to get through; the mob being inclined to be rude and jeer at us, especially when we had to dive under the stage. At last we got hold of a soldier, who understanding where we wished to go, took us to the consulate, where we fortunately found the vice-consul at home, who gave us dinner, bed, and breakfast. The next morning he escorted us clear of the city on our return to the boat, which we found at the place we had left her on the previous day. There were some fine shops in the town, which is a place of considerable trade. We found all the crew in the boat, because, being Cantonese, they said they did not wish to speak to, or to have anything to do with the Chinese of the village, beyond buying provisions of them, as they were pigs. It is curious to find how bitter the Chinese of one province are against those of another. A pull and sail of eighteen miles brought us back to the ship by another route after a very pleasant cruise, as Captain R—— was a first-rate travelling companion. Altogether we had made a circuit of nearly 100 miles, obtaining a very valuable knowledge of the country and inhabitants.

On the 22nd, the "Dwarf" left for the harbour of Takow, in the southern part of Formosa. When outside the river Han, we passed great quantities of fishing boats, one of them carrying a large Joss or idol, with flags flying, and priests and others beating tom-toms, shouting, and singing. It was apparently a religious ceremony, to induce Bhudda to give them good fortune. We sailed across leisurely, in order to exercise the ship's company at sea, and to sound the Formosa bank in different parts, as it was reported to have grown and altered considerably since the last survey. As far as we could discover, the chart was very correct; had there been any great alteration we should probably have found it out, as the weather was most favourable for our work. The bank is irregular in its depth, and the current runs over it with great strength, so that, even in fine weather, in many places there are overfalls, or broken water, that could easily be mistaken for shallow patches unless examined closely. In stormy weather there is a very dangerous sea on the bank; vessels should therefore avoid going over it at that time if possible.

We moored in Takow on the 27th. This harbour has a very peculiar entrance, looking as if an earthquake had rent off a portion of Apes hill to form an entrance, and let the sea into the lagoon behind. The entrance is very narrow, and has a bar of sand across it, and is only fit for small vessels to make use of it; the large ones anchor outside, where the anchorage is good in the N.E. monsoon, but very dangerous in the S.W., as it then becomes a lee-shore. At present, a good pilot can take vessels, drawing twelve feet, over the bar at high water. There are many apes and monkeys on Apes hill, overlooking the harbour on the north side, but they are very wary, and difficult to get at, as they dodge the sportsman from rock to rock, and, just before he can get a good shot at them, scratch themselves, and chatter, and bound away. A belt of flat, cultivated country, of nearly thirty miles in width, cuts them off from their kindred in the mountains in the interior. While here, the Rev. H. R——, of the London Presbyterian Mission Society, with whom I had become acquainted, asked me if I would like to accompany him on a visit to a village about fifty miles inland, where there was a chapel and a small Christian community of Peppohoans. I gladly availed myself of his offer, and with a party, consisting of his wife and two children, another lady, my servant, and myself, we started on the morning of the 29th of November. We first crossed the lagoon to the village of Ling-a-leau, where we got chairs with coolies for the ladies, and also coolies to carry our luggage and provisions; the rest of us walked to the district city of Pethou, about six miles inland, which has a magistrate, and about 6,000 inhabitants. There is a Christian chapel here, with a congregation of about sixty families. The chapel has three rooms attached, for the use of the missionaries or Chinese teachers, when travelling. As Mr. R—— had some work to attend to at this place, we remained for the night; and in the evening I accompanied him to visit a poor old Chinese Christian who was very ill and not expected to live. He appeared quite cheered by Mr. R—— coming to visit and pray with him. He said he felt at peace with God and man, and had a firm confidence in our Saviour. His wife was tending him most affectionately, and seemed in great grief for the state of her husband. A Chinese teacher lives at the chapel to perform the services, and to instruct those men, women, and children that wished to attend the school. The service consisted of hymns, prayers, and a portion of the Scripture, in the Presbyterian form of worship; the congregation appeared orderly and attentive. I may as well here mention that on subsequent occasions, when I have been on shooting excursions in the country, I have attended the service at some of the different native chapels on Sunday when no English missionary has been with me; and that I have always found everything carried on with the same order and decency as when one has been present. The next morning we left Pethou for the town of A-lu-kan, which was about twenty miles farther, in a N.E. direction. The country was flat, and supported a large population; it was well cultivated with rice and sugarcane. The villages have a dense wall of bamboo round them, and, as they look all alike, are very puzzling for a stranger to tell one from the other. We stopped at the house of a Peppohoan Christian, at the valley of Hoeng-sia, near A-lu-kan. His name was Ka-leng-hai, and he was a very fine old fellow, with a nice and pleasant wife and family of fine tall sons. He was an elder of the church at A-lu-kan, and well known to many foreigners on account of lodging them in his house, and accompanying them in their shooting excursions. His house was very prettily situated in a plantation of beetle-nut palms and bamboos, and was kept much cleaner than houses generally are in Formosa. The Peppohoans are the descendants of the savage tribes who inhabited the plain country in Formosa, and, who after being conquered by the Chinese, have mixed with them to a great extent. The Chinese like to have Peppohoan women for their wives, as they can do so much more work, being finer and stronger women than the Chinese. They do not contract their feet; and dress the hair differently to the Chinese women, twisting it in a plait round the head, with a piece of red cloth worked in the plait; altogether they are prettier as well as more useful. Mr. R—— was well known and evidently greatly respected; all the Christians we met by the way shook hands with us, and saluted us with the expression "Paheng," which means "peace be with you." Ka-ling-hai kept plenty of fowls, and had tried to rear turkeys, but the young ones had always either died from the damp in the rainy season, or been killed by small gnats or flies biting their eyes. The climate of Formosa does not agree with turkeys in any part, although they thrive very well at Amoy, which is much drier in climate and soil. The next day we continued our journey to Baksa, about twenty-five miles farther on. For the first fifteen miles or so, the country still continued level, and well cultivated with rice, sugar, sweet potatoes, and ground nuts; the villagers had also plenty of pigs, fowls, geese, and ducks; water buffaloes were used for ploughing and drawing carts, where the road admits of their being used, but they had very few other cattle. The people in the towns were mostly Chinese, but in the country villages Peppohoans began to get more numerous as we advanced inland. We crossed several rivers, some by wading, and others on rafts made of bamboo. The last part of the way was over a hilly country, very pleasant after the monotony of the rice fields on the previous day. Wherever we stopped for our meals, whether in the towns, villages, or at roadside inns, a crowd always collected round the ladies when they got out of their chairs, and examined their dresses and the children's. They intended no rudeness, although it was excessively inconvenient, but the ladies bore it very good-humouredly. When sitting in the chairs they could not be seen, as the chairs are fitted with bamboo blinds, so they were not noticed while journeying.

In a lovely situation among the mountains is placed the small village of Baksa, containing a chapel and school-house for the district round, which is mostly Peppohoan. The natives built them almost entirely at their own expense, the society adding a hut of mud and bamboo, consisting of three rooms, and a cooking shed for the use of the missionary on his visit. As the hut only cost the society eighty dollars, it was not a very extravagant outlay; it was made like the houses of the country, with a sort of outer wall of bamboo, about two and a half feet from the real wall, to prevent the rain from beating the mud-walls down in the S.W. monsoon. There were nearly 400 people at church on the Sunday I was present, but the greater number of these were only hearers, as the missionaries are very careful not to baptize too readily. Many of them could read the hymns, and New Testament, which are written in the Chinese character; and copies are also written with the Chinese words spelt with Roman letters as near the pronunciation as possible; as it is found that those that cannot read at all, will learn more quickly by using the Roman characters than the Chinese. A foreigner can easily follow them when singing the hymns from one of these books, though he may not understand the meaning of the words. While here, Mr. R—— and myself walked across the hills, about five miles farther to the Peppohoan village of Ka-ma-na, where there was also a chapel and a Chinese Christian teacher. We had a most beautiful view from the top of the range on our way, steep mountains on one side, and a long stretch of tableland and plain on the other.

On December the 4th, my Peppohoan friend Ka-leng-hai (who had accompanied us to Baksa) my servant, and myself, left Baksa and our friends to return to Takow by a route more inland, along the foot of the mountains. We reached A-lu-kan by night, and slept at Ka-leng-hai's house, and the next day got back to Takow, making a walk of fifty-five miles in two days without trouble. As far as

PEPPOHOAN WOMAN AND CHILD, BAKSA.

I could judge, Christianity is spreading more rapidly among the Peppohoans than Chinese, on account of their character being more simple, and their having no great attachment to the Bhuddist form of worship, which has only become known to them since their conquest by the Chinese. Also, as they are not rich enough to support many temples or priests to oppose the new faith, the work of conversion among them is like planting in a new soil. Formosa is also fortunate in having missionaries who appear to have their heart and soul in their work, without regard to bodily toil, or sickness from travelling in a climate that in some seasons is most trying on account of fever, ague, and dysentery, but the Almighty gives strength when needed to those that ask His help earnestly.

The hospital for natives at Takow, which is supported by the foreign community, is also a great means of showing the bright side of the Christian character, as any poor man who chooses to come, is doctored and fed free of expense, and on his return to his native village, cannot fail to give a good report of those who have treated him so kindly and generously. This pre-disposes the natives for the work of the missionary, and in many cases villages have sent in to request religious instruction, simply from the report of some of their people who have been to the hospital, and heard the Word of God preached while there under treatment for their bodily ailments.

Before any chapel or school-house is built, the natives of the district, to show that they are really in earnest in their new faith, collect sufficient money among them to build the chapel and school; and in some cases, where rich enough, contribute to the support of the Chinese teacher themselves.

CHAP. I.] *Absurd Stories against the Christians.* 31

The Roman Catholics also have a mission with a school attached, about two or three miles from Takow; and one at the foot of the mountains besides, which is about thirty-five miles inland. The Roman Catholic priests dress in the Chinese dress, and when once in the country, make up their minds to remain there for life and never to visit Europe again. They also have many converts.

Christian natives are occasionally annoyed by absurd stories being spread among the Chinese, it is supposed by the Literati, who are hostile to foreigners, in order to excite the people against them. These reports are generally to the effect that the Christians steal children and take out their eyes to make medicine, or other stories equally absurd. At one time while the "Dwarf" was at Takow, stories of this description had caused much excitement and ill-feeling among ignorant people in the interior; but it soon subsided when the representations of H.M. Consul caused the Chinese authorities to issue a proclamation that these stories were false, and only spread by wicked people.

Several of the officers had fair shooting near the harbour, pheasant, duck and snipe. We unfortunately lost one fine young man here; a stoker who had been on leave on shore with three other stokers, and had gone to the village of Ling-a-leau across to the side of the lagoon opposite to the town. As it was late when they wished to return, they could not get a sampan or Chinese boat, they therefore took a catamaran themselves, and tried to push her with long bamboo poles across the lagoon, which is about a mile and a half broad in that part, and about six or seven feet deep. It soon got dark, and began to blow hard. They first lost one pole, and then the other. As they had nothing else to propel the raft, one of them jumped after the pole that was sticking in the mud, and swam to it to bring it back. The tide and wind swept the raft from him, and as none of the others could swim, they could render no assistance. Shortly afterwards they got on shore, and ran into Takow asking for assistance, and then went on board their ship and reported the accident. Although all the ship's boats were sent away to search for the poor fellow immediately, and several of the merchants had started with their boats when the alarm was first given, yet they could not find him, and the body was not recovered for a week. It was buried in the cemetery after an inquest had been held, the captain performing the impressive ceremony, there being no clergyman at Takow at the time to do it.

Some of the merchants keep ponies which they

kindly lent to the officers to ride. The only good gallop is along the sand at low water, as the spit forming the lagoon and on which the town is built, is only a ridge of sand hills about eight miles long, and terminated by the rocky wedge-shaped hill called Saracen's Head. Some of the fishermen on this coast use a net of fine gauze stretched on a frame like a shrimp net, and pushed before them in the same way to catch a very curious little fish, less than half an inch long and quite transparent. They take them out of the net by a basin, and it is only after some little time that a stranger can see the fish at all. The first thing you notice is two little black specks, and then a little transparent body attached, darting about incessantly; the specks are the eyes. These little fish are sent up the country, and sold to rich Chinese to stock their fishponds, as they live in fresh water and grow to be good fish for eating.

On the 12th, the ship left for Tai-wan-foo, the capital of Formosa, which is about twenty-eight miles north of Takow by sea. It is situated on a small river, which is rapidly filling up with sand. The city is now about four miles from the sea, which formerly came close up to the walls, so that in the seventeenth century the Dutch and Chinese fleets could lay close to it; and for many years afterwards there was a good harbour for small vessels at Amping, which then became the port for Tai-wan-foo, but now there is only sufficient water for boats to cross the bar. The Dutch had a very strong fortress here, and one also at Tai-wan-foo, called Fort Zealandia, but both forts are now in ruins, having been taken from them by the Chinese Admiral Koxinga, in 1662, A.D. The Dutch only held Formosa about thirty years. It was at this place that more than one hundred Englishmen, who had been wrecked in the ship "Nerbudda" and the brig "Ann," were barbarously murdered in cold blood by the Chinese authorities in September, 1841, and March, 1842. We had several guests on board for the passage, and they had barely time to get on shore, before it commenced to blow so hard from the N.E. that there was no communication for two days, the weather becoming quite cold, almost freezing. The Consul, an officer of the ship, and myself, made an official visit to the Tauti or Governor of Formosa. He lives in a yamun in the city, to which we went in chairs of state, and were received with the usual salute of three guns, and a motley guard of Chinese soldiers, armed with spears and matchlocks. The Tauti was a very pleasant man, and gave us cakes, Chinese wine, and tea which is ceremoniously drank by guests and host when the visit is about to finish. He was unfortunately an opium smoker, and evidently suffered from the effects. He was formerly the Tauti of Amoy, and said he did not like his promotion, as they did not know how to make such good cakes in Tai-wan as at Amoy. Chinese wine is of the colour of indifferent light sherry. It

CATAMARAN, FORMOSA.

is drank warm, and is not unpleasant. The Tauti said that cold drinks were bad for the stomach. They have the same or rather a greater horror of cold baths. The next day I returned on board the ship through the surf on a catamaran, sitting in the tub, which just holds two people with much squeezing; the raft was paddled by four men. The catamarans are very buoyant, but sometimes capsize, leaving the passengers to float in their tub.

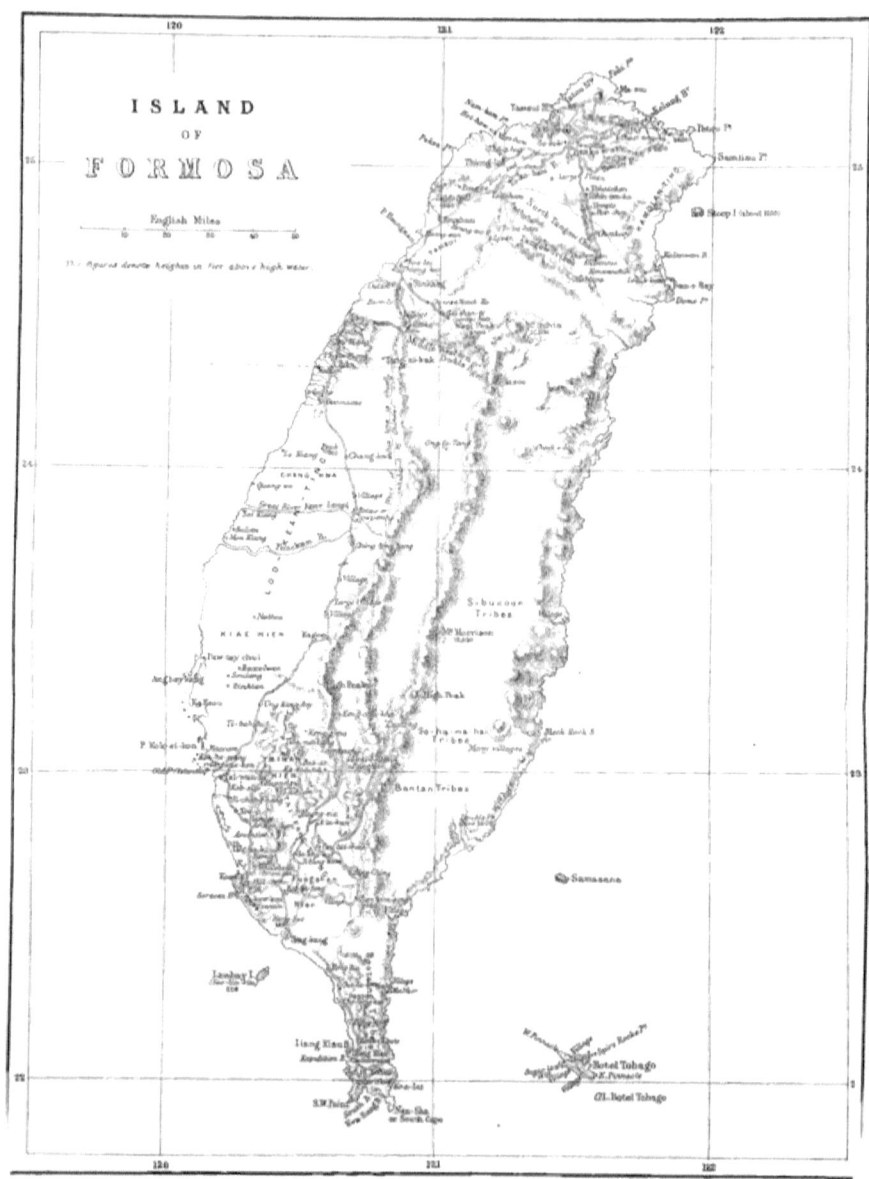

CHAPTER II.

THE HISTORY OF FORMOSA.

FORMOSA, "the beautiful island," as named by the Portuguese, has been recalled to notice by the recent insurrections there, and by the prospect that it may be destined hereafter to attract more the attention of foreigners. The Chinese name is Taewan, which signifies Terrace Bay. Its intrinsic and relative importance will justify us in recalling a portion of its history, and in exhibiting a brief description of the island. Its length, which is greatest from north to south, includes more than three degrees of latitude; its breadth, which is at most about eighty miles, is much narrowed towards each extremity. The channel which separates Taewan from the Chinese coast is from seventy-five to one hundred and twenty miles in breadth; in which, and about twenty-five miles from the island, lie the Pang-hoo or Pescadores islands. They afford good harbours, and were long the resort of Chinese pirates, and of the Dutch, who from this secure station could easily command the passages on both sides.

Though lying opposite to the Chinese coast, and within a day's sail of the port of Amoy, yet Formosa does not appear to have attracted the notice of the Chinese government till a modern date. According to their history, they had no knowledge of it till 1430 A.D., in the reign of Sueun-Tsung, the fifth emperor of the Ming dynasty, when an officer of the court was driven by a storm upon the island. More than a century later, a pirate who had been driven with his fleet from the Pang-hoo isles by a Chinese squadron, took refuge on Formosa. The island was then uncultivated, and inhabited only by savages. The pirate, who was an ambitious man, seized upon the island for himself, and the better to fit it for his purposes, massacred all the inhabitants that fell into his hands, smearing his vessels with the blood of the unfortunate natives. In some such way, doubtless, many Chinese must have gone over to Taewan before its occupation by the Dutch, which we now proceed to relate.

The early voyages of the Hollanders to the East Indies, says Burney in his Voyages, were projected by individuals or different companies, and prosecuted with the spirit of reckless adventurers. The Dutch East India Company was established in 1602. Nowhere was the mutual enmity of the Dutch and Portuguese more actively displayed than in these

Indian seas, where commercial jealousy was superadded to many other causes of animosity. Soon after the formation of their company, the Dutch began to contend with the Portuguese for the Chinese trade. The Portuguese successfully opposing their designs, the former in return besieged Macao in 1622, from which, however, they were repulsed with much loss. From the tenure by which the Portuguese held Macao, the Chinese regarded this attack as an act of hostility against themselves. But the Dutch accused them of aiding the Portuguese, and alleged as just cause of complaint, that they were admitted to trade on a fairer footing than themselves. Frustrated in their designs on Macao, they therefore sailed for the Pang-hoo islands. The Chinese having no sufficient force there, the Dutch took possession of them, and began a fort, to forward which many Chinese crews were condemned to labour. Of 1500 workmen thus employed, it is related that 1300 died in the progress of the building; "for they seldom had more than half a pound of rice for a day's allowance." The Dutch pleaded in vindication the cruel usage received by their countrymen, who had been imprisoned by the Chinese.

This establishment of the Dutch annoyed all parties; the Spanish, by rendering dangerous the commerce between Manila and China, the Portuguese, by interrupting the trade between Macao and Japan; and to the Chinese it was "an incessant and intolerable grievance," who therefore commenced negociations. The emperor required the preliminary step of their withdrawing from the islands; the Dutch claimed "nothing more than liberty of commerce with China, and the prohibition of it between the Chinese and the Spaniards in Manila;" nothing was effected, and the Dutch recurred to their former means of persuasion. Eight ships were despatched at one time to scour the sea and destroy whatever they could seize along the Chinese coast. Negociations were resumed, and the Chinese promised that if the Dutch would withdraw from the Pang-hoo islands they might fortify themselves upon Formosa without reprehension; a reasonable permission, no doubt, from them who had no right to the islands. In the year 1624 the Dutch concluded peace with the Chinese, by which liberty of commerce was granted them. They on their part evacuated the island, sailed to Formosa, and took possession of a harbour on the south-western side. The best entrance to it was narrow and shoal, there being at high water no more than thirteen feet.

Thus the Dutch entered upon Formosa, a small

Japanese colony then resident there soon retired, and the natives offered no opposition. To defend their new establishment, a fort and batteries were built, which protected the principal harbour, Takeäng; this fort was named fort Zealand. For the defence of the trade between China and Manila, the Spanish governor of the Philippine Islands fortified the fort of Kelung in 1626; from which, however, the Spaniards were subsequently expelled by the Dutch. Thirty miles from this harbour, on the western shore, another settlement was formed called Tam-shwny. Yet the jurisdiction of the Dutch extended little beyond the towns and villages in the neighbourhood of their principal fort. In these they wisely combined the Dutch and native authority; "they introduced new laws among them, and instead of their councils of elders, constituted one of their chief men supervisor in every village, who administered justice and was accountable to the governor of the island." The natives in these districts were reclaimed from many barbarous customs, and became attached to the government of the Dutch.

In 1626, George Candidus, a Protestant divine, was appointed minister to the settlement; and he took great pains to introduce Christianity among the natives. At the governor's request, he gave his opinion on the prospects of propagating the Gospel in Formosa. He considered both the dispositions and circumstances of the people favourable for their conversion to Christianity. "With good capacities, they were ignorant of letters; their superstitions rested only on tradition, or customs to which they were not strongly attached, and which had been almost totally changed within the last sixty years: no obstacles were to be apprehended from their government. God blessed his efforts in Formosa, so that during a residence of sixteen months, part of which was occupied in studying the language, he instructed 120 of the natives in the Christian religion." The number of Christians, it was found, daily augmented; the intermarriage of Dutch and natives was practised; churches and schools were multiplied, so that in all, many thousands of the islanders were converted to Christianity and baptized. "But the Dutch governors in India were cautious of encouraging the conversion of the Formosans, lest it should give offence to the Japanese, with whom they had commerce, and by whom Christianity was then heavily persecuted." Thus, as often elsewhere, the interests of true religion were sacrificed upon the altar of Mammon, and the knowledge of salvation withheld for money.

The whole interval of Dutch authority in Formosa was a period fraught with calamity to China, both from the scourge of civil war and foreign invasion. In 1644, the Mantchou Tartars had gained the capital, Peking, and the Tartar chief was acknowledged as Emperor of China by most of the northern provinces. At the close of the next year, twelve of the fifteen provinces had submitted to the usurper. Throughout the whole course of this long war, the Chinese were emigrating to other countries, to escape the miseries of their own. Early in the struggle 25,000 families are said to have transported themselves to Formosa. The industry of these strangers gave the island a cultivated appearance, and increased the produce of rice and sugar for exportation. At first the Dutch encouraged this immigration, and at length were unable to prevent it; which influx of foreigners aided in the final overthrow of the Dutch dominion in the island. But the unexpected and unheard-of result, that of Europeans being defeated in contest with the Chinese, will excuse a minute description, and demands a brief retracing of some previous events.

These calamitous and turbulent days produced in China, as ever elsewhere, some daring spirits, who rode upon the storm, and whose names are well known in the history of those times. None of these was more remarkable than the half-piratical, half-patriotic naval chief, Ching Ching-kung, better known as Koxinga. His father was once a servant of the Portuguese at Macao, and was instructed in the Christian religion, and baptized by the name of Nicholaus. From a petty trader, he grew, by foreign trade, to be the richest merchant in China; and afterwards equipped, at his own expense, a small fleet against the Tartars. His success gradually drew around him a vast number of Chinese vessels, till he became commander of as formidable a fleet as ever sailed these seas. But, after many battles, the Tartar chief invited him to court, and offered him the dignity of king, which he accepted, leaving the command of the fleet to his son Koxinga, whilst himself was doomed to perpetual imprisonment at Peking. Koxinga, with more than his father's valour, opposed the usurper, and continued faithful to his country. During several years he scoured the seas with his formidable fleet, descended upon the coast, and, with the aid of a land force, retook some cities, and defeated the enemy in several engagements. But in three or four years the Tartars, by force and bribes, recovered all, and drove him from the coast to the numerous islands which line the shore. In this state of affairs, the larger and fertile island of Formosa became the object on which the exiled chieftain rested his last hopes. The Dutch foresaw the danger; they were aware that the agents of Koxinga held secret correspondence with the resident Chinese; and the garrison at Fort Zealand was accordingly increased in 1650. For several succeeding years there was no open hostility, and Koxinga being fully employed against the Tartars, neglected Formosa; yet dissatisfaction was mutually increasing between the Dutch and the chief. But after his severe defeat in the siege of Nanking, he had no resource left but to obtain the island; his followers were dispersing to procure subsistence, and his fleet could not be kept together. He now began to look in earnest at the "beautiful isle." The Dutch also increased their vigilance; took some of the most considerable emigrants as hostages, arrested and tortured others who were suspected. At the earnest request of Cozet, governor of Formosa, twelve ships were despatched from Batavia in 1660, with large reinforcements, and orders that if the alarm at Formosa proved groundless, the fleet should proceed to Macao. The garrison at Taewan now consisted of 1500 men, a force which the admiral thought superior to any number whatever of Chinese troops. A categorical answer was demanded of Koxinga, " whether he was for peace or war ? " The wily chief replied by letter, that " he had not the least thought of war against the company." To remove suspicion, he sent several merchant ships to Taewan; but as he still continued his vast preparations for war in his stronghold at Haëmun (Amoy) and Kemun, the governor's suspicions were not removed. The majority of his council, however, were of opinion that there was no present danger, and all the ships were therefore ordered away to their respective places. The admiral returned to Batavia, and accused the governor of unreasonable apprehensions. The council, wearied with the expenses, and with the false alarms of the governor for several years, suspended him from all office, and ordered him to Batavia to defend himself. M. Clenk, his successor, sailed for Formosa in June, 1661.

Widely different from these conjectures were the events then passing at the island. No sooner had the Dutch fleet departed, than Koxinga and his forces were in motion. He embarked 20,000 or 25,000 of his best troops in a great number of vessels, and appeared before Fort Zealand, and, assisted by thousands of his countrymen on shore, began to land. He first stationed a number of his vessels between Fort Zealand and Fort Province, on the opposite side of the entrance, and occupied with his forces a point which would cut off the communication between the forts.

The governor seeing this, ordered out 240 men to dislodge the enemy from this post. Here was the first trial of their strength. By the time of their coming up, 4,000 Chinese had already occupied the place; but so confident were the Dutch that the enemy would not stand the fire, that they immediately attacked them. "But so far were the Chinese from giving ground, that they returned the fire with musketry and arrows, and sent a detachment to attack us in the flanks. This alarmed the soldiers, who threw down their arms and fled, leaving the captain and nineteen men to the mercy of the enemy. One half only of their company reached the fort alive. Nor was the defence by sea any better. The four ships in port attacked the junks, and sunk a few; but one of the four was burned by the Chinese fire-ships, and the rest escaped from the harbour, to which they all returned again but one, which sailed away for Batavia." By passing around the Philippines, she reached Batavia in fifty-three days; the first instance of a passage down against the monsoon. The Chinese landed without any further opposition, and in four hours' time cut off all communication between the forts, and also between Fort Zeland and the open country. Koxinga now summoned the fort, threatening to put all to fire and sword, if they did not surrender immediately.

A consultation was immediately held, and it was agreed to send deputies to Koxinga, offering to surrender Fort Province rather than to lose all. They went to his camp, then consisting of about 12,000 men, who were besieging Fort Province. They were armed with three different sorts of weapons; the first, of bows and arrows; the second, of scimitars and targets only; and the third, of backswords and pikes, three or four feet long, with broad pointed irons at the ends. The deputies were conducted into a spacious tent, where they waited till Koxinga was at leisure. He meanwhile was employed in combing his long shining black hair, a great ornament among the Chinese. "This done, they were introduced into his tent, all hung with blue; he himself was seated in an elbow chair, behind a four-square table; round about him attended all the chief commanders, clad in long robes, without arms, and in great silence, with a most awful countenance." Koxinga replied, that Formosa had always belonged to China, and now the Chinese wanted it, the foreigners must quit the

Surrender of Fort Province.

island immediately. If not, let them only hoist the red flag. Next morning the red flag waved over Fort Zealand, but Fort Province was surrendered with all its garrison and cannon.

To prepare for a more vigorous defence, all the men able to bear arms were taken into the fort, and the city set on fire, but not so effectually as to prevent the Chinese from preserving many of the buildings which afforded them a shelter. They also brought up thither twenty-eight cannon to bear against the fort; but they were so galled by the fire of the Dutch, that the streets were covered with the slain, and the besieged making a successful sally, spiked the enemy's guns. Koxinga now finding all his attacks fruitless, began a close blockade, and meanwhile made the open country feel his rage. He made the Dutch, especially the ministers and schoolmasters, prisoners, because they were suspected of secretly encouraging their parishioners to kill the Chinese residing among them; some were crucified by the Chinese, and their crosses erected in their respective villages. One individual case of this kind, as related by Mieuhoff, is so Regulus-like, that we present it entirely to the reader.

"Among the Dutch prisoners taken in the country was one Mr. Hambrocock, a minister. This man was sent by Koxinga to the governor, to propose terms for surrendering the fort; but in case of refusal, vengeance would be taken on the Dutch prisoners. Mr. Hambrocock came into the castle, being forced to leave his children and wife behind him as hostages, which sufficiently proved that if he failed in his negociations, he had nothing but death to expect from the chieftain. Yet was he so far from persuading the garrison to surrender, that he encouraged them to a brave defence by hopes of relief, assuring them that Koxinga had lost many of his best ships and soldiers, and began to weary of the siege. When he had ended, the council of war left it to his choice to stay with them, or return to the camp, where he could expect nothing but present death; everyone intreated him to stay. He had two daughters within the castle, who hung upon his neck, overwhelmed with grief and tears to see their father ready to go where they knew he must be sacrificed by the merciless enemy. But he represented to them that having left his wife and two other children in the camp as hostages, nothing but death could attend them if he returned not. So unlocking himself from his daughters' arms, and exhorting everybody to a resolute defence, he returned to the camp, telling them at parting, that he hoped he should prove serviceable to his poor fellow prisoners.

"Koxinga received his answer sternly: then causing it to be rumoured that the prisoners excited the Formosans to rebel against him, ordered all the Dutch prisoners to be killed; this was accordingly done, some being beheaded, others killed in a more barbarous manner, to the number of 500, their bodies stripped quite naked, and buried fifty and sixty in a hole; nor were the women and children spared, many of them likewise being slain, though some of the best were preserved for the use of the commanders, and the rest sold to the common soldiers. Happy was she that fell to the lot of an unmarried man, being thereby freed from vexations by the Chinese women, who are very jealous of their husbands. Among the slain were Messrs. Hambrocock, Mus, and Wenshaim, clergymen, and many schoolmasters, who were all beheaded."

Thus ended that tragical scene.

Two days after the council at Batavia had censured Coyet for his fears, and had dispatched his successor Clenk to Formosa, the "Maria" arrived with the news from Formosa. They immediately revoked the censure and suspension, and fitted out ten ships with 700 soldiers for the island; but Clenk arrived first off Taewan, where instead of the rich and peaceful station he had flattered himself with obtaining, he saw the red flag flying, and hundreds of Chinese vessels lying in the northern roads. He anchored in the southern, sent his despatches ashore, did not land himself, but sailed for Japan, and was heard of no more at Formosa. Soon the succours from Batavia arrived, and the besieged began to act on the offensive. They were unsuccessful, however, in attempting to dislodge the enemy from the city of Zelandia, and suffered the loss of two ships and many men in the attempt; the garrisons were now ordered from the two northern ports, Kelung and Tamshwuy to increase the force of the besieged. The women, children, and other useless persons were also sent to Batavia." These preparations checked the approaches of Koxinga for the present, which led to an injudicious act on the part of the besieged. The governor received letters from the viceroy of Fuhkeën, requesting his co-operation in expelling the remains of Koxinga's forces from the coast, and promising his whole aid afterwards to the Dutch at Formosa. Five ships were therefore dispatched for this purpose, but three were lost in a storm, and the remainder returned to Batavia.

This act was just to the wish of Koxinga, and

led the besieged to despair of holding out much longer. A deserter from the Dutch encouraged the besiegers, and directed them where to press the attack. They now assailed the port from three near batteries, and notwithstanding opposition, after many assaults, succeeded in making a breach. Then the besieged began to deliberate, and the majority of the council agreed that the fort was untenable. The governor yielded his opinion to the majority, surrendered the public property, but was allowed to embark their private property for Batavia in their only remaining ship. Thus, after a siege of nine months, the loss of 1600 men, the Dutch returned to Java; "where the governor and council of Formosa, after all the hazards and incredible hardships they had undergone, were imprisoned, their goods confiscated, and the governor condemned to perpetual banishment in one of the Banda Isles—but was finally recalled by the Prince of Orange." Thus, after thirty years' duration, ended the Dutch authority in Formosa, in 1662.

Freed from all opposers, Koxinga now distributed garrisons throughout the western parts of Taewan. and established an undisputed dominion there. He constituted himself sovereign of the island, assumed a princely style, and fixed his palace and court at Zelandia. Then the island assumed a new aspect; for with their proverbial industry he introduced also the Chinese laws, customs, and form of government. He even looked beyond "the beautiful island" to the rich clusters of islands which almost bordered on his narrow domain. He had threatened the Philippines and was preparing for an expedition against the Spanish there, when he was arrested by death only two years after his gaining Formosa, and left his possessions to his son. Ten years after, when the provinces of Kwang tung and Fuhkeën revolted against the Emperor Kanghe, this son resolved to join the king of Fuhkeën, but not being acknowledged by the latter as a sovereign prince, he declared war against the king on the spot, defeated him in several battles, and weakened him so that he was obliged again to submit to the emperor and receive the tonsure. Kanghe now abolished the title of king, and appointed a governor over Chekeäng and Fuhkeën. This man seized upon the Panghoo Isles, and proclaimed general amnesty to all who submitted to the emperor. This policy had the desired effect of inducing many Formosan emigrants to return to China and of weakening the enemy upon the island, till it was finally surrendered to Kanghe by the grandson of Koxinga. Thus ended the sovereignty erected by that chief, and Formosa passed into the hands of the Chinese government in 1683.

Little change ensued in the government or customs upon this change of masters. The imperial authority on the island though often assailed by insurrections during the last 150 years, is still maintained. The lands possessed by the Chinese in Formosa were at that time divided into three districts; the subject natives composed forty-five towns or villages. Little can be said with certainty of the events which have since transpired there.

The two most prominent events are the destructive inundation in 1782 and the rebellion in 1788. The official report of the former disaster states, that in May (which is not the month for typhoons) a wind, rain, and swell of the sea together for twelve hours, threatened to overwhelm the island. On its cessation, the public buildings, granaries, barracks, and salt warehouses were found totally destroyed, and most private houses were in ruins; of twenty-seven ships of war, twelve had disappeared, and left not a piece of wreck behind. The emperor directed that all the houses thrown down should be rebuilt at his expense (*i.e.*, from the public treasury), and provisions supplied to the people. "I should feel much pain," said he, " were one of them to be neglected." Subterranean convulsions may have conspired with the winds to aggravate this calamity.

This event was followed six years later by the most important and bloody rebellion which Formosa has yet witnessed. The particulars cannot be given, but its suppression by cruel punishment and almost indiscriminate proscription, tarnished the name of Keënlung the emperor. M. de Grammont states in a letter of March, 1789, that the troubles on Formosa are ended at last, but at the cost of a shameful and expensive war to China. She has lost at least a hundred thousand men, destroyed by disease or the sword of the rebels; and she has expended more than two millions of taels. The only advantage that she has secured is the recapture from the Formosans of the two places they had seized. According to the returns of the Chinese general to the emperor, the renowned rebel leader, Lin Chwangwan, has been captured and cut into a thousand pieces; but according to private advices the rebel still survives, and the real sufferer was only a Formosan bearing the same name.

THE CAPTURE OF AMOY BY THE MANDARIN FORCES, 1853.

CHAPTER III.

THE NEIGHBOURHOOD OF AMOY—JOURNEY UP THE NORTH RIVER—
DRAGGING A SCHOONER OFF THE BEACH IN FORMOSA—VISIT TO
THE MISSION STATIONS S. W. OF AMOY—THE FOO-CHOW STATION
—KELUNG—SAU-O-BAY—THE LOO-CHOO ISLANDS—TAM-SUI.

On the 14th of December the "Dwarf" sailed for Amoy, and arrived there the next evening having had to steam up close inshore on the China coast for a short distance, as the N.E. monsoon was too strong to allow her to fetch across with sail alone. The wind generally moderates when close inshore; small vessels therefore always creep up along the land when the N.E. monsoon blows very strong. They also avoid the current, which runs the same way that the wind blows in the Formosa channel.

At Amoy this time I met the Rev. Dr. T——, an American medical missionary, whom I knew when I was a midshipman in a brig in 1853, during the dreadful massacre that took place at that time when the city was taken by assault by the Imperial troops, from the rebels after a long siege. On this occasion the massacre had become so revolting, that even round the two English men-of-war that were lying in the harbour, they were cutting off heads and throwing people overboard from the junks, and then spearing them in the water from boats, as if it were by way of amusement. At last our people became so enraged at the sight, that it was put a stop to on the water with a strong hand, by the interference of the British consul, and the commanders of H.M. ships "Hermes," and "Bittern." They sent their boats to prevent further bloodshed by taking the Chinese prisoners out of the mandarin junks, and giving them safety on board their own vessels and a merchant junk, to the number of nearly 700 people. Although the slaughter was stopped on the water, it was still going on in the city, where the government troops were butchering men, women, and children, without regard to their belonging to the non-combatant part of the inhabitants; the real rebels having fled in their junks in the morning as the government troops climbed over the walls. At that time Dr. T——was living in a house outside of the foreign settlement, where we had a guard of marines for its protection; the merchants' houses being all on the side of the harbour near the city, and not on Kulangsue island as at present; and the settlement was further protected by having a gate at each end to prevent the Chinese from entering. At the risk of his life, he went into the street near his house and gave shelter to fugitives from the scene of bloodshed. I well remember being sent to him with a message about the wounded men in his house, and seeing the floor of every room, as well as the verandah, covered with Chinese hacked about in a dreadful manner. I believe about sixty were there. He took care of and fed them for several days, until they could be sent to a place of safety in company with those that were rescued by Her Majesty's ships. They were all eventually sent to that part of the main-land which was still in possession of the rebels, where they would be in safety. On the mandarin admiral being asked the reason of this great massacre of townspeople, he said that as they had been so many months capturing the city, and having killed so few rebels during the siege, it was necessary now they had taken it by assault, to report a sufficient number of killed to the emperor to prevent themselves falling into disgrace.

On Christmas Day we had the usual service on board, and the lower deck was very tastefully decorated by the ship's company, and the tables well spread with good cheer. Everyone appeared to enjoy himself much, and the men were pleased to see many ladies and visitors from the shore to look at their decorations, and walk round the lower deck with the officers, tasting the pudding, &c., while the banjee played the "Roast Beef of Old England."

On the 27th of December, a party of us went with two covered boats to examine the rivers near the town of Hai-têng, about eighteen miles from Amoy. This was an important city once with two walls, and in some places even three, all of them being about twelve feet high and six feet wide. On the outer wall not far from the river there was a pagoda, which was probably built for a watch-tower. The effect from the top of this pagoda looking over the interior of the city was very strange, as the houses have been so long destroyed that the trees among the ruins have grown to a great height, and the few houses now inhabited have the appearance of hamlets among trees and fields.

Hai-têng was first destroyed by the Tartars in 1660, but was afterwards rebuilt. A rebellion broke out here, and it was thoroughly destroyed by the mandarins when they took it about the year 1854, and most of the people who could not escape were killed. In sieges by the Chinese, the walls of the cities often suffer little, but after the cities have fallen, the houses inside are pillaged and destroyed. It is quite saddening to anyone who travels much in China to see the number of cities in this desolate state. The country round Hai-têng is very fertile with rice fields, and is studded with villages. The hills are rugged and barren; some of them run abruptly down to the plains, and

PUMPING WATER INTO THE RICE-FIELDS.

are covered with tombs. In the alluvial soil at the base of the hills, great quantities of peaches, oranges, and pomelloes are grown. The plains are intersected with canals, and it is difficult for a stranger to find his way about. We also examined the north river as far as the Tang-kang bridge, about twenty miles from Amoy. This bridge was built during the thirteenth century, and is composed of very large blocks of stone; some of them measured fifty-five feet long, and five feet square at the end. Near the junction of the river there is a large town called Chor-bey which has a considerable junk trade, as the cargoes from the large sea-going junks are transferred here to smaller boats to be carried up the river. It is painfully dirty, and has open cesspools in the streets, making the air most offensive. Notwithstanding this, people say that the town is usually very healthy; open cesspools are not considered so dangerous by the Chinese as closed ones. We also visited some of the curious square castles built by the Tartars about 1660 A.D. to hem Koxinga in, who had possession of Amoy and the country round for about thirty miles, and who held it against all their forces for many years. The castles are now in ruins; they were built a few miles apart, extending from Red Bay on the south, nearly to Chinchew on the north. There is a Protestant mission chapel at Chor-bey, and one also at Pechuia, which is a far cleaner town than Chor-bey, but with less trade. A seven storied pagoda, made of stone, stands on the top of the Nanti-shan mountain and forms an excellent landmark for vessels bound to Amoy; the mountain being 1720 feet high, can be seen a very long distance. I could find no record of the date when this pagoda was built. A few stones mark the site of a temple and fort that were close to it. Tradition relates that the fort was built about 200

B.C. by a king of this part of China to overawe the natives. It is a stiff walk to the top, but the view well repays the trouble of climbing there.

On New Year's Day every one visited his friends. It seemed a very sociable custom, and I was told the American part of the community originated it at Amoy. The Chinese are very punctilious about their own visits at the Chinese New Year's Day, which is kept as a holiday, and also several days after. All debts have to be paid by the New Year, and to prevent incurring the dishonour of not doing so, those in debt sell or pawn their goods very cheaply a short time before. The Chinese New Year falls later than ours, and each year the day which will be kept is notified beforehand by the mandarins.

The Amoy races came off on the 9th of January, and were very good fun. They were run by ponies, some of which went capitally. Our doctor rode, and won two races, much to the delight of all our bluejackets that were present, who, of course, had backed their own officer. After the horse, or rather pony races, there were foot races, and running in sacks, which afforded great amusement.

There is a curious rocking-stone in the garden of a joss-house in the suburbs of Amoy, weighing about five or six tons. The priests are glad to exhibit it, and place a cup of water on the stone to show the motion when you give it a good push.

There are great quantities of graves outside the city, and also small tombs for the bones of those

POTTED ANCESTORS, AMOY.

that have been collected and placed in earthen pots.

Some of our officers had tolerable duck shooting about six miles from the town; there were also plenty of wild geese in the neighbourhood, but very wary and difficult to get near, unless you put on the straw coat and hat of a Chinese boatman, and crept up to them in a sampan, as they appeared to take but little notice of the natives. One evening our ship's company gave a Christy Minstrel entertainment at the club, which had been kindly lent them by the residents for the occasion. As we had several good actors among the men, it afforded great amusement to our guests.

On the 13th, one of the officers and myself started in the whale boat with four men, having the skiff in company, which we took it in turns to pull or sail, and in which were placed some of our sleeping things. We examined the short cut, or passage, to the North river, and then ascended it till we got beyond the first rapids, which are about sixty miles from the city of Amoy. Every night we encamped on the bank of the river under a tent made of a sail spread over the boat's mast, and secured by oars to the necessary height. The men slept in the boat, as they preferred to coil up in her under a tarpaulin. We had a spanking breeze with us, and sailed up nearly all the way, passing under the Tang-kang bridge, which I have described before. A fleet of large tea boats accompanied us, and were on their return from delivering tea at Amoy. Before dark we always anxiously looked out for a dry place to camp on, as the twilight was short. Although we found the country people very civil, we avoided the villages as much as possible in consequence of the crowd round the fire to see Jack cook, to smell, and make remarks on the savoury dishes; and afterwards when eating our suppers it was difficult to keep elbow room, so eager were they to see everything. Beyond this, we experienced no rudeness, but on the contrary we sometimes found them very obliging; for instance, on one occasion we got short of charcoal for cooking, and on my asking one of the Chinese to get some more for us, he went away, and returned in a short time with a basket full of it, and would not take any payment whatever. We found the current of the flood tide to extend only about three miles above Tang-kang bridge; beyond that the current running down was merely ckecked, and caused the water to rise while the flood tide was making below. The country for the first fifty miles consisted of flat fertile plains or valleys, hemmed in by mountains. Rice, sweet potatoes, and sugar were the usual crops; but in some places there were deliciously cool looking groves of orange trees, and pomelloes which gave a most agreeable shade. A range of mountains comes down close to the Tang-kang bridge, but after passing this range there is a splendid rich plain, till you arrive at the " Gorge," which is about thirty miles beyond.

Here the cliffs come down perpendicularly to the river, which is so narrowed by them that it looks as if the mountain had been cleft asunder by some great convulsion to make a channel for the water. The current in the Gorge runs very fast, and it is difficult to stem it. Although the tea boats were so crowded together here that collisions were frequent, yet the greatest good humour prevailed among the crews, who carefully kept their boats from hurting their neighbour's by pushing them apart with long bamboo poles, and were particularly attentive in preventing our whaler or skiff from being hurt: the latter gave them great amusement as she sailed along like a perfect toy with her small triangular sail, and kept up with the large boats with little difficulty. The river is very deep in the Gorge, but shallow where it widens in the plains. After passing through the Gorge there is another level valley, but smaller than the last one; after a few miles the mountains commence again, and the whole country from this place gradually rises, and causes a succession of rapids in the river. Most of the towns and villages have a castle or fort for the natives to drive their cattle into, and to take refuge in themselves from any attack by another village. These feuds are of constant occurrence; in fact, a blood feud is hardly ever made up again. Polam was the largest town we passed. It is about forty miles from Amoy, and is a thriving place, in consequence of the cargoes being transferred from large boats to be distributed over the country by small flat-bottomed ones drawing very little water. Some of the rapids took a long time to ascend. With our boats, we had to get out and pull them up, walking alongside. The large tea boats were tracked up by a rope from the mast, the majority of the crew pulling on the end of it from the towing-path, the rest pushing from the boat with long bamboo poles shod with iron—at some places the crews of several boats united to get them up one at a time. Where the water admitted of it, and the current was strong, we also tracked our boats up.

The first part of our return journey was quickly made, and the sensation when shooting down a rapid was very exciting. The rest of the journey was not so pleasant, as we had a hard pull against a very strong breeze, with disagreeable rainy weather.

On the 20th of January, the ship ran over to Formosa under sail, and anchored off Takow. The anchor was hardly down before an officer belonging to the British consulate, and another gentleman, came on board and requested assistance for a schooner that had run on shore about twelve miles to the southward. We weighed immediately under sail, and soon ran down to the schooner and anchored close to her. It was a sandy beach where she was, with a nasty surf running on it. The captain who came on board on a catamaran said that his vessel had been drifted close to the beach in a fog, and that on his seeing the surf, he had tried to put the schooner's head off from the shore, but there being little wind at the time, she had drifted into the surf before he could let go his anchor, which he had done directly he found he could not get her head round. On this coast the lead gives little warning, the water shoals rapidly after you once get ten fathoms of water, and in some places this would be only a short distance from the shore. Vessels should therefore be very careful in approaching this part in thick or foggy weather. The schooner was a new vessel and very strongly built with iron knees. She had no cargo on board, only stone ballast. The captain and myself landed to examine her, as he thought she was driven too high up on the beach to get off again. She was nearly broadside on the sand, with only one foot of water at her bow, and three feet at the stern. When afloat she drew seven and a half feet, the rise of tide would be about three feet, and it was low water when I landed. About 200 or 300 natives and Chinese were waiting patiently on the beach for the crew to desert her, so that they might pillage without any opposition. The crew had evidently made up their minds on the subject, as they had all their clothes packed, ready to leave her. I noticed that every time a heavy sea struck the stern, the vessel lifted a little; I therefore concluded from this that she might be got off, by bringing a very heavy strain on her so as to pull her stern round a little every time she lifted. Having sounded carefully from the schooner to the "Dwarf," we weighed and moved in to three fathoms water, where we anchored, and then, by means of catamarans, the surf being too heavy to use our boats with safety, we got two large hawsers from our stern to that of the schooner, and veered our ship in as close as we could with safety. Everything being ready, and all the ballast having been taken out of the schooner, we steamed ahead, at first slowly, then with the full power of the engines, the ship's company heaving on our cable at the same time. At last the hawsers carried away, and we could do nothing more that tide. As the weather remained fine we tried again the next day, having taken up a better position with the "Dwarf;" we also hired a quantity of Chinese, to assist by coming on board the "Dwarf" and hauling on a tackle secured to our cable. At last when the tide was at its greatest height, the stern of the schooner began to move round a little as each wave struck her. This made us redouble our efforts, till the stern was towards us, when she made a sudden start off, to our delight and the disappointment of all the expectant pillagers, who disappeared over the sand hills in a few minutes. We towed her to Takow in safety, and on examination found she had not been strained at all, being so well built. Although the schooner was saved on this occasion, yet I was sorry to hear on the last visit I made to Takow, that this vessel had been caught in a typhoon in the Formosa channel in 1873, and had foundered with all hands.

We remained at Takow a few days and then visited Swatow, and after that went to Amoy again, calling in at the Chinese town and harbour of Tong-sang on our way. It is a walled town and must have been a place of great importance once, although it is very poor now, with but little trade. A Buddhist priest came on board and offered to pray to Buddha for a fair wind for the ship, or anything else anybody wanted, in consideration of a small gratuity. I do not think he was much patronised on board the "Dwarf," although he showed some very curious certificates, given him by other vessels that had patronised him.

We arrived at Amoy on the 23rd of February, and the next day the consul and myself visited the Chinese admiral on official business. He was a fine old Chinaman, and held the rank of commander-in-chief of sea and land forces in this district. He was zealous in the service of his country, and notwithstanding great opposition from other officials, improved the Chinese war junks very much, by putting copper on the bottom of them, and supplying them with chain cables and iron anchors like foreign vessels, instead of those of wood with a large piece of stone fastened to them like they had before. This took place before the Chinese government had commenced to buy and build steamers themselves, and when the originator of any innovation ran a great risk of falling into disgrace. We afterwards called on the Tauti, or civil governor. The Yamuns of both these mandarins were very spacious, with one court opening into another, planted with trees and flowers, and having many birds and other animals in cages, gold fish in ponds, and also grotesque figures carved in stone. The rooms were very draughty, and during our interview, the soldiers and retainers remained in the hall below the dais (or upper end of it), very similar to the description of a nobleman's reception in the middle ages in Europe. Tea, wine, and cakes were served, and pipes also produced.

On the 6th, the Tauti returned my visit on board the "Dwarf." He made most minute inquiries about the cost of the ship in stores, wages for the crew, provisions for a month, and also about the quantity of coal consumed for the speed and distance done. Whatever information he obtained was noted down by an official, I believed as some sort of an estimate of what ought to be the expense of keeping up their own gun-boats, which they find very costly. The next day the Chinese admiral came on board; he examined the guns and arms most minutely, and seemed very intelligent by the inquiries he made.

In consequence of the great increase in the number of coasting steamers of late years, the large junk trade that formerly existed at Amoy has become considerably reduced. From the appearance of those that still remain, and from the very indifferent crews they have, it is easy to believe in the very heavy loss of junks that takes place in the typhoon season, or even in strong N.E. gales. The crews are merely shipped for the voyage, and the great proportion of junks are old and so worn out that it is a matter of surprise they can get any one to go to sea in them. By the chin-chining joss and beating of gongs that take place on their sailing, even on the shortest coasting voyage, and the great rejoicings that take place on their return, they evidently fully appreciate the risk they run.

While at Amoy this time I accompanied the Rev. Mr. M., of the Presbyterian mission, to visit some of their stations in the district S.W. of Amoy. As far as the town of Pechuia we went in a house boat belonging to the society, fitted up with two sleeping places. After this we changed into a smaller boat for ascending the river to a village called Kwar-jem. As the weather was warm and pleasant we slept very comfortably in the boat. We passed numbers of cargo and passenger boats on the river, and the fields were quite alive with labourers cultivating the rice, and men, women, and children pumping water from the river into the fields by chain-pumps worked by treading with the feet, like a treadmill. When the water in the creeks gets too low for cargo boats to float down, the crews of several of them unite in making a dam across the stream a short distance below the place where the boats are. This collects the water in the stream till the boats float to the dam, which they then break through; and when the boats ground again they make another dam, and so on until they get into deep water. Although this is a slow process, it is not so slow as one would imagine, on account of the boats being flat-bottomed and drawing little water.

At Kwar-jem there is a tower for the defence of the villagers; it is square, with a court in the centre, and rooms all round, and is several stories in height. The village is large and dirty, and has a Protestant chapel in it. From this place we walked to a village called Thir-bouy, about eighteen miles inland in a S.W. direction, where we put up at a chapel belonging to the mission, which has two rooms attached for the use of the minister. It is situated in a valley between the hills, and has a mud wall round it. The people at all the villages in the country seem very simple and quiet, not near so restless and annoyingly inquisitive as those in the towns. We passed few villages on our route, which led over rocky hills covered with scrub, and there was but little cultivation to be seen.

At about nine o'clock in the evening, as I was sitting at the open window thinking what a peaceful, quiet looking place this village was, after the bustle of the ship and the port, suddenly all the animals—dogs, cats, pigs, and cattle—set up their own particular noise to the utmost extent; even an owl joined in the din by hooting as loud as possible. Suddenly a woman screamed, and every villager that had been outside the house dashed in and shut doors and windows as quick as possible. Presently one or two of them ventured out here and there, and then Mr. M. came in and said a tiger had been in the village, but had left again without doing any damage, as everything was fortunately under shelter. The village soon returned to its usual quiet state; but this did not last long, because about half an hour after out dashed all the men from their houses, and rushed frantically out of the village. This proceeding was caused by a watchman giving the alarm that thieves were stealing the potatoes in their fields. They were successful in catching one man from a neighbouring village, whom they bound and brought in in triumph. The Chinese steal potatoes and fruit from each other so frequently, that every field of any size has a watch-house, built of straw or bamboo, just large enough for a man to lie in and look out for thieves. For this reason it is difficult to get good fruit, as it is picked and sent to market long before it is ripe, to prevent its being stolen. My illusions concerning the peacefulness of the country villages in China were thus rudely and effectually dispelled. Of late years tigers have increased very much in this district, and often make a raid into a village, carrying off pigs and dogs. I was informed that within a radius of ten miles, on an average, a man, woman, or child was carried off every month by the tigers. In the previous year, when Mr. M. was returning by a night journey, a tiger must have followed his party through the hills, because they passed a roadside inn about daybreak where they had noticed a woman lighting the fire to prepare the rice for early travellers. (The fire is generally outside the inn, with a large boiler over it.) The woman was carried off soon after they passed, and no traces of her were found.

On Sunday there were about 120 Chinese at the chapel, some of whom had come from a long distance, bringing their dinners with them. Many of the men nursed their little children, and did it very well. They formed a very attentive congregation, many of them could read the service, and all joined in singing the hymns fervently.

At 1.40 A.M. on the 18th we commenced our return journey with several coolies and other people who wished to go with us, as a large party gives greater safety. Mr. M. gave a short but impressive prayer before starting; and as it was quite dark, with no moon, we had torches of pine to light us on the way and scare the tigers off;

altogether the effect was very strange as we travelled along the mountain paths in single file, from the fitful glare thrown by the torches on the Chinese, the rocks, and the trees overhanging the path.

On the 23rd of March, the ship left for Swatow. We sailed down quietly with light variable winds until we got to the Lamock Islands, where we lay becalmed. At about 7 P.M. a mist appeared in the N.E., which came down rapidly on us with every appearance of bad weather; sail was taken in and the position of the ship carefully noted. At 8 P.M. the squall struck us with great violence, and perfectly blinding with rain, making it very difficult to run through the islands and anchor in a safe place for the night. The next morning we got to Swatow, and finding everything quiet in the neighbourhood sailed across to Formosa, where we arrived on the 10th of April. On anchoring at Takow, I was informed that a junk had arrived from the Pescadore Islands, and reported that a vessel was on shore there. At the same time the news arrived that the steamer "Hailoon" was on shore on Breaker Point on the China coast. As the Pescadore Islands were the nearest, we went to Makung at once, the principal town of the group, and the residence of a mandarin, to whom we took letters from the mandarin at Takow, requesting him to give us every assistance and information about the wreck. On communicating with this official, he assured us that no wreck had occurred for a long time, and that if any had taken place it must have been reported to him at once. At the same time our own people had a good look round for any signs of wreckage or plunder, but found none; we therefore concluded that the story was caused by some mistake about the wreck of the "Hailoon" on the China coast, to which we then proceeded.

We found the "Hailoon" on the beach, and H.M. ship "Elk," and the steamer "Formosa" anchored off her. They were endeavouring to make her seaworthy, by building a bulkhead or sort of dam across the bow where the hole was, to prevent the water from coming into the body of the ship. In this they succeeded, and eventually took her down to Hongkong in safety. Her accident was caused while steaming up the coast against a strong N.E. monsoon, and consequently keeping close in shore. She had struck on a pinnacle rock which had about twelve feet of water on it, and which was not marked on the chart or known before, except by the Chinese fishermen, who knew of its existence by the trouble it caused them when their nets got entangled with it. These people afterwards pointed the position out to the officer who was sent to examine it. When the steamer struck on the rock, and the captain found the water flowing in, he backed her off and then ran her up on the beach as far as possible, to save the passengers, crew, and cargo. He had then gone to the nearest Chinese official, who sent off messengers for him to obtain assistance, and also sent a guard to protect the wreck.

As we found our services were not required we proceeded to Amoy.

On May the 2nd, information was brought that the steamer "Douglas" had run on the Dyoyu rocks near Namoa Island. We immediately went to her assistance, and found the steamer "Quantung" anchored near her. The "Douglas" had run on the rock, while going so fast that there was no hope of backing her off and saving the vessel. She had a large hole in the bottom, and the tide flowed over the stern as well, when we arrived. The Dyoyu rocks are very rugged and in an exposed position in bad weather, so that there is little chance of saving a vessel that runs on them. The "Quantung" had taken ninety-seven boxes of treasure from her, each box containing about 4,000 dollars. Chinese from the shore were employed to dive and hook the boxes on under water. As the rest of the treasure was lower down and at the bottom of the vessel, from twelve to twenty feet under water, and as the Chinese divers had left in consequence of the weather getting stormy, some of our men volunteered to dive and recovered ten boxes containing 40,000 dollars. We had no diving dresses and therefore it was very arduous work. The decks were cut through as much as possible, and two oars were lashed together to guide the men down and up again, and to prevent their rope getting entangled with anything and drowning the diver.

The captain of the steamer informed me that, after getting on the rocks, they were attacked by Chinese, who came in boats from the shore, which was about five miles off. They had much difficulty in driving them back, and had to fire on them repeatedly, the officers, crew, and passengers behaving very bravely. Soon after they got on shore they had been able to send to Swatow, which was about thirty-five miles off, to report their disaster, and the "Quantung" had been sent to their assistance immediately, but she left the day after the arrival of the "Dwarf." Junks to hold the cargo were sent from Swatow, and when the weather permitted Chinese coolies and divers came from the shore to save cargo in company with our people. It was very dull and monotonous work, but was occasionally enlivened by Chinese trying to come close and pilfer. On one occasion, on the 6th, we noticed eight large Chinese boats coming off slowly before the wind, with apparently few men in them: when about a quarter of a mile from the wreck we saw a number of men start up, who shouted, brandished spears and knives, and waved flags—they must have numbered between 300 or 400 men. Commencing to pull towards the wreck, they evidently intended to board and plunder. As we always kept ready for this sort of work (this place having as bad a reputation as any in China for piracy), we threw a shot from the twenty-pound rifle gun across the bow of the first boat. Seeing they paid no attention to this, the gunner made a beautiful shot just over one boat which splashed another nicely; this shot falling so well, effectually showed them that we would stand no nonsense, and they all turned round and made for the shore. By the old custom of China any wreck is considered the property of the nearest villagers, and a rush is made for pillage, as was formerly done in England as well as other countries many years ago; a Chinese junk has no chance if wrecked, and the crew are only too glad to escape with their lives. Knowing this custom made us more anxious to drive them off without bloodshed than if we were certain they were regular pirates. After nineteen days the cargo was all cleared out, and the vessel stripped of everything of value, so we went to Swatow and landed the captain and officers of the wreck. On our way to Amoy, a few days after, we passed close to her, and found she had almost entirely disappeared in a gale.

The captain's statement of the reason of his losing his ship was, that the appearance of the land in the evening had deceived him so much, that he did not think he was so far from the mainland and out of his course. While anchored at this place I constantly watched the appearance of the mainland and Namoa Island, and noticed that sometimes one would appear quite close, and sometimes the other, though both were about five miles off. This showed the necessity of constantly taking cross bearings when coasting in China to avoid being deceived.

We were at Amoy during an eclipse of the sun on June 6th. The Chinese commenced beating gongs, and drums, blowing horns, firing guns, and making as much noise as possible, to frighten away the monster that was eating up the sun.

As I wished to see some of the mission stations

on the North river near Amoy, and the Rev. Mr. M. of the Church Mission Society had kindly said I might accompany him, we started in a mission boat on the 7th, and got to Polam the next night. On our way we passed a village where they were holding the festival of the Dragon boat. Three long boats, richly painted and gilded with a dragon's head at the bow, were paddled by crews of twenty men each, and raced down the stream; gongs were beating, flags flying, and a crowd of women and children yelling and shouting; it was a very pretty sight, as the village was situated among beautiful green fields of rice and sugar-cane, and groves of orange trees and pomelloes, with a range of mountains at the back. I attended the chapel at Polam on Sunday, and there were about fifty people present; very few of these were baptised Christians, the rest were only hearers. The Chinese teacher was a fine-looking man and had a curious history. He had formerly been a petty military mandarin, and commanded a war junk in Formosa, where he had a sharp fight with some pirates. In the action a stinkpot was thrown on board his junk, which exploded and a piece wounded him in the eye, and he was also badly burnt. He suffered great agony from his wound, and the Chinese doctors could not cure nor even relieve his sufferings. His friends therefore wished him to go to the foreign hospital for Chinese at Amoy. For a long time he would not go, so great was his hatred to foreigners. At last the great pain he suffered compelled him, and the English doctor managed to give him relief at once, but the sight of one eye was quite gone. While in the hospital he heard one of the missionaries preaching in Chinese. The text was "Lay not up for yourselves treasures on earth," &c. This roused his attention, and he began to think there might be some good in foreigners and their religion, and that they might not all assist in debasing his countrymen by selling them opium, but that there must be many good and charitable men to support the hospital and to skilfully treat people without receiving payment for it. After his wounds were healed he left the hospital, and by this time had become a zealous convert to Christianity. On rejoining the military service he began to preach his new faith, and in consequence soon got into trouble, and at last had to choose between giving up his rank in the army or his religion. He chose to give up everything for his faith, although from the bravery he had shown in battle there was every probability of his becoming a high mandarin. After some time he qualified for and became a teacher at the chapel at Polam, where he zealously performed his duty and lived on his small salary.

There was another interesting case at Polam of an old man who had been an astrologer, and had made a comfortable livelihood by predicting lucky days for marriages, the proper position to build houses in with regard to the direction of the doors and windows so as to bring good fortune to the possessor, and various other superstitious practices. On becoming a Christian he was no longer allowed to make his living by these means, and being very old had a very hard struggle to earn his food. Finding it very difficult to refrain from returning to his magic arts when pressed by hunger, as he could easily make a fee of three dollars by doing so, he gave his astrologer's compass to Mr. M. to take away and thus remove temptation from him.

On the 12th of July information came that an American gentleman employed by an English firm at Takow had been knocked down, wounded, and robbed, by some Chinese near that place. As there was no United States ship at Amoy, or Takow, the "Dwarf" went across in case there should be anything seriously the matter, or the chance of a disturbance. On arriving we were told that this gentleman had been travelling in a chair with four Chinese coolies from Tai-wan-foo, the capital, to

Takow, which was about thirty-seven miles by land; he was travelling by night on account of the heat. When he had gone a little more than half way his coolies were stopped, and he was told to get out of his chair, and on his doing so, he received a blow from a spear across his head which stunned him and made a nasty wound. When he recovered his senses he found himself surrounded by many Chinese robbers, who took everything from him, and a box containing the books of the house, which could not be of any use to them, but were very important to the firm. They had evidently expected that he had treasure with him, as the boxes which hold about 4000 or 5000 dollars were generally sent down from Tai-wan without any guard when it is necessary to send it away to Amoy, in consequence of it being very dangerous to embark it at Tai-wan-foo on account of the surf.

He had no treasure with him on this occasion, so they were disappointed and left him lying very still, apparently dead, on the road. When the robbers went away, his coolies picked him up and carried him into Takow. There being no American consul in Formosa the British consul had immediately taken the matter up and seen the Chinese officials on the subject. After some few days the mandarins managed to recover the books and secure two of the thieves by means often resorted to in China. A magistrate went to the village which was the nearest to the place where the robbery had taken place, and made the head man of the village responsible for the recovery of the plunder and capture of the robbers. On the head man expressing his inability to do either of these things the magistrate seized his brother and put him in prison, telling the head man that if the books were not recovered in three days he would flog his brother with bamboos. The books were not found in the time named, the brother therefore received a beating with bamboos, and the head man was informed the dose would be repeated if they were still not discovered. After this the villagers set to work, and at last found the box with the books all right inside, buried in a field. The brother was then released, but the magistrate put a "squeeze" or fine on the village for not catching the thieves, although they protested the robbers did not come from their neighbourhood, but from the capital, and that they had returned again. As the "squeeze" was to be increased if no one was caught, at last two men were produced for being implicated in the robbery, and were tried and punished. The Chinese officials showed no reluctance on this occasion to administer justice.

On the 9th of August we were relieved from the duties of senior officer on the Amoy division and transferred to those on the Foo-Chow division, which was the next station farther to the northward, and where we accordingly went; after relieving the "Avon" we remained at Foo-Chow till the 27th, when we visited Kelung harbour in Formosa. This harbour is situated on the N.E. end of the island, and is the only harbour in Formosa that is deep enough for large vessels to make use of. In strong N.E. winds a nasty sea rolls in, and it is very unsafe in the typhoon season, although vessels have ridden out typhoons there, yet many have been lost. The safest anchorage for small and light draught vessels is in nine or ten feet of water, where there is a soft muddy bottom and well sheltered behind the reef that lies opposite to the custom-house.

There are generally several steamers and foreign vessels loading here, the coal mines being conveniently situated in the hills, from three to four miles from the harbour. The coal is worked by Chinese, no foreigner being allowed to hold a mine or do more than mere agency business. The Chinese pick the coal out of the side of the hills, where it crops up, in the most primitive manner, as they have but little enterprise or knowledge of mining on a large scale. Coolies are employed to bring the coal down the mountains in small baskets; some of it is placed in small and leaky open boats at Coal Harbour, which is about five miles off by sea. On its passage along the coast to Kelung, it generally gets well wetted by the spray and waves washing over the sides of the boats. From other mines it is sent down the Kelung river in boats of a similar description, arriving in nearly as bad a state, as it constantly rains at Kelung, and they never cover the coals. From this treatment, as well as in consequence of its being of an inferior quality, Kelung coal is much disliked, wet coal being a dangerous cargo to keep on board ship. It was very cheap, being from fifteen to seventeen shillings a ton, to which must be added an export duty of four shillings a ton on coal sold to merchants, but this tax was not required from war ships. Should the Chinese Government allow foreigners to work the mines, the coal would probably be put on board in a much better state, and possibly of a better quality by working deeper. A tramway could easily be made from the mines to the harbour, a distance of three or four miles, and arranged so that the laden trucks going down should pull the empty ones up. There is a reef most conveniently placed near the custom-house on which a wharf might be built for embarking the coal and sheltering the lighters. There are plenty of fish in the harbour, which the natives try to catch at night in nets, placing fires on the bows of their canoes to attract them. These canoes are in such numbers that the lights stretch right across the entrance to the harbour, making a strange and pretty scene on a dark night, with the reflection on the water and the high land at each side of the entrance.

We remained here for a few days, and then went on to a large bay, about fifty miles to the southward, called Sau-o-Bay, which is on the border between the Chinese and savage territory. It is a fine bay, but open to the east, and therefore unsafe in the typhoon season, except for junks and very small gun-vessels that can anchor behind the reef at the end of the bay. A Chinese village is built by a small river, and has a slightly cultivated valley around it. Everywhere else the mountains and hills come close down to the water. On the savage side they are densely wooded; but those hills on the Chinese side are bare of trees, not only on account of cultivation, but also to deprive the savages of the advantage of attacking them by crawling up under cover of the forest, which is their favourite mode of fighting. A few farms were scattered about the valley at the head of the bay, but the farmers had to go to their work in the fields with their weapons ready for use, and keeping one man on the look-out to give the alarm. Many of the fields nearest to the savages had evidently been uncultivated for some time on account of their savage neighbours.

There were two villages of Peppo-hoans on the south side of the bay, which were carefully protected by stockades of bamboo, and had a watch-tower near the centre, as they also sometimes suffer from the attacks of the savages. In consequence of the crews of vessels that are wrecked on the east coast of Formosa being always ill-treated and often killed, I was desirous of making some arrangement with the tribes to be kind to foreigners who were thrown into their power, and to forward them on to the Chinese, who would send then in to the nearest consulate, according to the treaty. An English gentleman belonging to the Chinese custom service, and who was stationed at Kelung, and had come as my guest to this place, was also anxious to accomplish the same object. We therefore landed with his Chinese servant, and tried to get a guide at the Peppo-hoan villages, but unfortunately without success, as they said they had a feud at present with the nearest savage tribes, and any of their people would be killed if taken by them. The Chinese, of course, refused to go, as they were always at open war. We therefore went to the Chinese farm that was nearest to the border, and obtained information from the farmer of the way to the savage villages. After leaving him, we soon passed the cleared land, and at last got into the bed of a watercourse leading up the ravine between the hills. We scrambled on for some distance, the wood getting thicker as we advanced, but could find neither natives nor huts, so returned disappointed. When near the farm again we met our friend the farmer, who had called out all his army, consisting of nine men, armed with matchlocks, spears, long knives, and shields, and was marching to our assistance, as he had thought, from our long absence, that we had got into trouble. Although we felt grateful to him for his anxiety to rescue us if necessary, it was difficult to keep from laughing at the appearance of the motley array.

While the ship was at anchor here a great number of men, women, and children from the Peppo-hoan villages came on board to see her. The women were very nicely dressed in jacket and trousers, with a sash round the waist, and having their hair done up in a plait and tied round the head. They were not at all shy, but chatted and laughed together at what they saw, and rolled up rough tobacco leaves and smoked the rudely-made cigar with an air of great pride. On their leaving the ship some one happened to throw a bottle overboard, at which several of our fair friends jumped into the water and swam after it with all their clothes on. For the rest of the afternoon our people amused themselves by throwing empty bottles for the ladies to swim and scramble for, and small coin for the men to dive after, which they did wonderfully well, not being encumbered with much clothing like the ladies.

The tea-plant grows here very luxuriantly, also rice, tobacco, sugar, sweet potatoes, and groundnuts. On the savage side, the camphor trees commence; they are very large, with huge trunks, looking quite grand in the forest. When cut they give out a very pleasant smell of camphor. These trees are gradually diminishing, on account of the wasteful manner in which the camphor is obtained, and unless some measures are taken to plant other trees, the forest will be gradually destroyed; the Chinese not only cut them down as they encroach on savage territory, but also send strong parties into the woods to cut them down on the savage territory, and distil the camphor from the small branches, the rest of the tree being left to rot if it is far from the sea or the means of transporting it.

We moored inside the reef, but found little room even for our small gun-vessel. Snipe abounded in the marshes near the beach, and pheasants and deer inland. Our people caught a few fish with the seine in the bay, and enjoyed cooking them for supper by a fire on the beach, and wading about in the water after the warm day. On the 5th of September, we sailed for the N.E. part of our station, as the ship's company were suffering much from the heat of the summer, and it was considered that a cruise at sea would be of benefit to them. We passed near to the different rocks and islands of the chain that runs from the north of Formosa, towards the Loo-Choo group, giving a good look at them in case there should have been any ships wrecked on them, and also to certify their position, because many of them are put down as doubtful on some of the charts. We also sounded at intervals to try if we could get bottom, and noted the current, which we found very variable in its strength, and always setting in a N.E. direction. Some of the islands are thrown up in a most abrupt manner, and are evidently of volcanic origin. As we had particularly fine weather, we were able to confirm the accuracy of Commander Bullock's observations on disputed cases.

On the 10th we put into the Loo-Choo islands, and anchored off the town of Napa-kiang, in the small bay called Barn-pool. In the afternoon three Loo-Choo officials came off, two of whom could speak a little English. We had tea, wine and cakes in the cabin, and, after the usual civilities, they inquired the reason of our visit. On being informed that we wanted fresh provisions, they requested that a list should be given in Chinese of what was required, and then everything would be sent off by their Government. After seeing the list and arranging about the provisions, I requested permission for the officers to land and see the country, which they said they could do after a little hesitation. When they left the ship two of us landed with them, and walked to the house of one of the gentlemen, in a village not far from the landing-place. The people appeared most polite, every one we met on the road bowing profoundly; they were curious to see us, but were not at all rude like the Chinese are. They were dressed like the Japanese, but the hair of the men was done differently; they do not shave the head, but tie the hair up in a bunch on the top and fasten it with a small silver arrow, instead of the top-knot of the

Japanese. The houses were like those in the Satsuma province of Japan, which are generally cleaner and neater than those in the other parts of the empire. Each house has a courtyard with a wall round it, which has a hedge of the banyan tree cleverly trained along the top. Farther in the country the courtyards had no wall, but only a hedge of evergreen round them, which had the opening before the door so arranged by a short piece of evergreen planted inside the opening and overlapping it, that no one passing on the road could see into the courtyard or house. The houses were raised off the ground, and were fitted with sliding panels instead of walls, so that if there were many visitors all the partitions could be made to slide back, the house becoming one large room, with only one little apartment left for the women, who do not appear when company are present. We had tea and cakes with our friend, and a great number of people came to visit us and to satisfy their curiosity.

The next morning before daylight, in order to avoid all bother and attendants, some of us landed clear of the houses and walked straight across the country to the capital of this group of islands, which is called Scheudi. It is situated on the top of a low hill about four miles inland, and was a very nice walk in the cool morning, along paths kept perfectly clean, and having hedges of well trimmed evergreens planted on each side. These evergreens have a pretty little white flower, and the leaves are of a very bright green, like orange leaves. Near the town the country became undulating, and highly cultivated with sweet potatoes, maize, millet, sugar-cane, tobacco, and rice. There were also some large temples and gentlemen's houses, with trees and grounds laid out round them, like a park in England; but the temples bore the appearance of having been much neglected. This pretty and quiet scenery was most refreshing after the glare from the scorched-up hills of China. The capital was very clean, each house being detached from its neighbour, the temples and gentlemen's houses being tiled, those of the poorer classes thatched. There was an old fortress on the top of the hill, but the gate was locked, and we could not get inside or make any one hear. We saw no guns or soldiers there, but had a most beautiful view as far as the sea on both sides of the island. We were in the town so early that the people looked as if they had only just got up; they came out of their houses to stare at us, and looked as surprised as if we had dropped from the skies. They crowded round while we were in the town, but were quite civil, and did not approach us within five or six yards. We met a school of young Buddhist priests on the road, wearing long yellow dresses, and carrying books under their arms. On our return to the boat, that was waiting at the proper landing place, we found a large crowd assembled, and also an official bearing a letter from the king, and a present of a pig, some fowls, sweet potatoes, and a few other vegetables, which he had kindly sent us. This official, and many others, came on board to examine the ship and guns. In the afternoon the beef and vegetables, that had been ordered for the ship's company, were sent off to the ship, the charge being very moderate; the beef was excellent, the best we had tasted since leaving England. The bullocks are very small, and the horses also; the fowls have a very gamey flavour. Before leaving I sent a letter of thanks to the king for his hospitality and presents, and also a present of blankets, serge, pictures, and books, which appeared to be as acceptable to his Majesty as his gifts were to us. The junk trade is carried on at the town of Napa-kiang, which is smaller than Scheudi, and possesses a close and safe harbour, with a very narrow entrance to it, well adapted for junks and fishing-boats, but too small for foreign vessels. There were only a few trading junks in the inner harbour, and they were dismantled. This town is not near so clean as the other towns, and the houses are built more like Chinese than Japanese, there being many Chinese living in it. The Loo-Choo officials seemed very anxious for us to leave the island, and always contrived to send one of their countrymen with us wherever we went, under the pretence of acting as a guide, and to secure us from any rudeness on the part of the natives. On landing, or on leaving the shore, we always found one of the three gentlemen who first called on us, professing to be delighted to see us on each occasion, but repeatedly saying that their island was very poor, possessing no gold, silver, copper, or coal in it, and growing barely enough corn and food for themselves, as if they thought we wished to annex the island, and therefore endeavoured to make it appear of little value. None of the shopkeepers would sell us anything, but when we came in to buy they made a precipitate retreat by the door at the back, and left us in the shop by ourselves; they evidently must have had orders on the subject. The burial ground for foreigners was near the landing-place, and was kept in good order, had a hedge round it, and was shaded by trees. One of the tombs has the following inscription, " Wm. Square, seaman of H.B.M.S.

History of Loo-Choo.

'Alceste,' was buried here, Oct. 15, 1816. This monument was erected by the King and the inhabitants of this most hospitable island." There were tombs for French seamen, the dates 1846 and 1848, and of ten men of the United States squadron that was here and surveyed the islands in 1853-4; and some others that I could not make out.

From the early records it appears that in the fourteenth century the Loo-Choos consisted of three petty kingdoms, and that they were united under one in 1430 A.D. The first intercourse with Japan took place in 1451. About 1600, they broke off intercourse with Japan, and sent tribute to China instead. In March, 1609, Shimadzu, a relative of Prince Satsuma, who owned the southern province of Japan, conquered the island and took the king prisoner, and kept him so for three years. Shimadzu received the northern portion of the Loo-Choos as a gift from Iyeyas, who was the tycoon of Japan at that time, as a reward for his services. After this, embassies were sent to Japan on the accession of every sovereign, and to Pekin as well. The Loo-Chooans have always been noted for their extreme courtesy, and call their island "the country that observes propriety." They send tribute to China twice in three years. The junks that bring the tribute are dismantled on their arrival at the city of Foo-Chow, the rudders are unshipped and landed, and the crews live on shore till the arrival of the next tribute junk. The junks that brought the former tribute are then allowed to return. This is done because the Chinese are afraid that Loo-Choo would cease to pay tribute if they did not keep the junks and crews as hostages till the arrival of the next. Captain Basil Hall, R.N., gives a very good description of the Loo-Choos in his book; and they have altered little in manner and customs since his time, 1816. The Rev. Mr. Bettleheam, who resided there for over five years, complains in his letter of September 1849, written in the Chinese Repository, that they sometimes treated him rudely in their efforts to get rid of him. When the "Dwarf" was there, no foreigners were on the islands. One or two vessels were wrecked on them in the last few years, and the crews represented that they received the kindest treatment from the natives. We saw no soldiers or weapons of any description, although they must possess them, as there is a fort at Napa and another at Scheudi, and they had wars formerly. The officials carried only a fan. There appeared to be no extreme of wealth or poverty, and the people seemed happy and contented.

The harbours and islands were well surveyed by the United States squadron in 1853-4. It is a valuable survey, as the channels between the reefs are very intricate. It was while attending on this squadron that our three Loo-Choo friends learnt the little English they knew.

We left under sail on the 12th, with a fresh S.E. wind, and in the evening killed the pig that had been presented by the king. During the night we had very unsettled and disagreeable weather, the wind coming in heavy squalls, and suddenly changing from one side to the other, with torrents of rain. The topsails were close reefed, and the frequent changes harassed the watch by compelling them to brace round constantly. Sometimes it lulled quite calm between the squalls. Several of the old seamen said the next day when the weather cleared up, that it was all on account of killing a pig at sea!—there being an old superstition that it was bad luck to do so. On our arrival at Tamsui on the 17th, we were told that a typhoon had passed Formosa, which must have crossed not far from us, and caused our bad night.

There are hot sulphur springs in the mountains about eight miles from the town of Tamsui, which are in a state of great activity; but the mandarins do not allow the sulphur to be worked, as they fear to disturb the "Fung-shui," or the Dragon that sleeps under the Celestial Empire, by scratching his skin in obtaining it. Notwithstanding this prohibition, there are evident signs that the sulphur is sometimes taken by the Chinese by stealth. In the neighbourhood of the springs there are some very pretty groves of parsamum trees around the farm-houses. The parsamum tree bears a luscious red fruit, which is very pleasant when fresh, and also when it is properly dried. A great part of our ship's company walked out to see the sulphur springs, taking their dinners with them, so as to make a regular pic-nic of it under the trees, and enjoyed themselves much.

CHAPTER IV.

WRECK OF THE YEDDO—MONASTERY ON THE CUSHAN MOUNTAIN—DISTURBANCE AT TWA-TU-TIA IN FORMOSA—VISIT TO THE SAVAGE TRIBES IN THE INTERIOR—FÊTE AT THE ARSENAL AT FOO-CHOW.

ON our return to Foo-Chow I visited the Chinese Arsenal at Pagoda Anchorage. It was under the superintendence of M. Giquel, who was formerly a lieutenant in the French Navy. It was kept in capital order, and would do credit to any European nation. The plant of machinery was excellent, and they made nearly everything required for their steam navy, and built very fine and fast gun-vessels, which were well adapted for the coast of China. The officers were trained in a naval college under English and French instructors. A training barque was attached to the college, and was commanded by an English naval officer, who took the cadets to sea and taught them the practical part of their education. The Chinese seamen were also trained to their guns and rifles. Those vessels that had good officers were kept in fair order, and were smart at gun drill.

If the Chinese gun-vessels were commanded by men that their crews had confidence in, they would be very formidable, as they have good speed and were well armed. Those that had been built at Foo-Chow were sharp forward, and according to the French lines. The machinery and boilers had been made at the arsenal, but some of the heavy parts had been brought from Europe. They also made their own chronometers and compasses. The leading men were French, but the workmen were Chinese, who carried out what they were told to do very well.

The "Dwarf" sometimes went up the river to the city of Foo-Chow-Foo, and moored a short distance below the bridge, which is solidly built of stone. The river near the city is divided into two branches by "Nantai" Island, on which the foreign settlement is built. The deepest channel at present is north of this island, but it is shoaling gradually every year. A great many years ago, the Chinese say that the deepest channel was on the opposite side of the island. The bed of the river is constantly altering, on account of the soil being light and alluvial; so much so that the Chinese pilot who is employed to take the gun-vessels up (which draw only about eight and a half or nine feet of water) makes a practice of sounding the river the night previous, and of placing marks made of a bush tied to a bamboo, which is stuck in the mud at the worst places. Even with this precaution there are several days, at neap tides, when there is not sufficient water. Large ships anchor off Pagoda Island. While on our way to Formosa, we went to sea by a channel at the entrance of the river called Round Island Passage, which we surveyed, as it cut off about seven miles for vessels coming up from the south; but the channel is shallow and intricate, and should only be used by a small gunboat on an emergency, and then only when the flood tide has half made. It might be useful in war to cut off an enemy's vessel.

The walls of the city of Foo-Chow-Foo are about five miles round, and are well worth the trouble of walking on, and the view from the top of the pagoda-shaped guard-house at the north gate is very extensive. The greater part of the land inside the walls is cultivated, as Foo-Chow has suffered from war, and been ruined like other Chinese cities. Before getting to the city, from the river, it is necessary to traverse about three miles of suburbs, in which some of the shops are fine, but the smells are vile. The Viceroy of the province of Fokien lives at Foo-Chow, and also the Tartar general commanding the troops, of which there are usually a good many in the city ready to be sent to Formosa, if necessary (as that island is under the command of this viceroy), or anywhere else where they may be required. The Imperial gun-boats built at the Foo-Chow arsenal are also under his orders. Each viceroy is expected to put down rebellion in his own province without assistance from the central government if possible. The quarrel with the Japanese which afterwards took place became so serious at last that the central government had to send troops to Formosa from other parts of the empire, the viceroy not having sufficient power to deal with it. The Japanese, the same as other foreign nations, in their complaints, made the Pekin Government responsible for the acts of their subordinates in any part of the empire. No viceroy or mandarin is allowed to hold an appointment in his native province, for fear of his becoming too powerful and causing rebellion by being too closely connected with the people.

On the 8th of October we left Foo-Chow to render assistance to the "Yeddo," a large iron steamer that had run on shore, on a reef off one of the islands to the south of the Haitan Straits. She had grounded at the time of high water, and at low tide you could walk nearly quite round her; the rise and fall of tide being seventeen feet. When she first got on the rocks, the Chinese fishermen had attempted to board and plunder her, but had been very gallantly driven back by the captain, officers, and crew, and also the passengers. As she was only about seventy miles from Foo-Chow, and in the track of steamers going up the coast, information was soon brought of her disaster, and the passengers sent away. The "Dwarf" remained by her for fourteen days, and transferred her cargo to another steamer. The wreck being then sold, as it was considered by the owner that the expense of repairing the holes and floating her off would amount to more than her value, we left her in charge of the purchasers, who had brought an armed junk for her protection. The yits, or islands, all around looked quite bare, as they had no trees or grass on them. They were inhabited by fishermen and a few farmers, who grew sweet potatoes and ground-nuts, a very poor-looking population indeed, to whom a wreck must be a perfect godsend. We returned to Foo-Chow by the Haitan Straits, making use of the Wilson's Channel, and we found, with care and attention, that there was little difficulty, the chart being very accurate. It ought to be a cause of pride with naval men to find how accurate the charts are on this very intricate coast, when we consider that

Captains Kellet and Collinson had no steamers or steam launches to take the full advantage of calm days for their surveys, and must have been constantly bothered by a fiery N.E. monsoon.

There are some very large and curious Buddhist monasteries near Foo-Chow. The largest one is built nearly half-way up the Cushan Mountain, which is about 3000 feet high, and lies between the city and Pagoda Anchorage. It is kept in good order, being a place of great sanctity, and a favourite shrine for Chinese pilgrims. There are a great number of priests attached to it, who are dressed in long grey coats, like the Roman Catholics, with a cord round the waist. These perform the service in the morning and evening, which consists of chanting the same words over and over again in a most monotonous manner, occasionally getting up from their knees and walking round and round before the idols, beating a gong and tinkling a bell; about fifty of them attend these services. During the service one of the priests places a small quantity of food on a stone pillar outside the temple for the birds to eat. The idols are very large, and richly gilded. It is situated in a sort of basin in the mountain, and possesses cool and pleasant walks under fine large trees, and has gardens and fish-ponds attached to it, and there is also a water bell placed in a stream, which gives out a very sweet tone. The priests ought to lead a happy life, if a fine climate, with a beautiful and quiet home and little work to do, can give it. There are some rooms attached to the temple which the priests let out to foreigners, who wish to live here for a change of air in the summer, and to get away from the great heat of the city. From the top of the mountain a most extensive view is obtained of the large plain round the city of Foo-Chow, which is well cultivated, and gives a good idea of the cause of the wealth that the city possessed in former years. This rich plain, which has the river flowing through it covered with junks and boats, the city, towns, and villages scattered about in all directions, and the mountains in the distance, makes up a picture that well repays the trouble of climbing so high to see. The tea-plant is grown in small patches about the sides of the Cushan Mountain, but the principal tea district is some miles farther inland.

Another very curious monastery is built in a large cave, which is situated in a deep ravine between the mountains on the banks of the You-en-fou river. The span of the cave across is 200 feet, and there is a deep chasm immediately under the temple, which is about 1,000 feet up the mountain.

Although this temple is of great sanctity, and the resort of many pilgrims, yet there are but few priests belonging to it. These keep the temple in order, preventing the trees being destroyed, so that the walk up to it is beautiful and shady, although it is a stiff pull up the steps leading from the bottom of the ravine. The usual way to go to this mountain from Foo-Chow, is in a house boat up the river to the foot of it, and then by walking up the mountain to the temple. The house boats are fitted up with every luxury for gentlemen and ladies to live on board of, as they sometimes go away in them for several days; the gentlemen to shoot, and the ladies for change of air and scene.

On the 16th, Vice Admiral Sir C. Shadwell, K.C.B., hoisted his flag in the "Dwarf," and steamed to the city of Foo-Chow from Pagoda Anchorage, where he had arrived in the "Salamis," which drew too much water to go further up the river. The races took place while he was there. They were very good, as the Chinese ponies have plenty of go in them. The course is about four miles from the settlement, and on the opposite side of the river to it. The race committee very hospitably entertained the officers at luncheon, and gave a good dinner to any of our ship's company that were present on each day, some of whom kept the course clear for them. The day's races concluded with jumping in sacks, and foot races between the blue-jackets and marines, which gave great amusement to the spectators. There were numbers of Chinese present who appeared to take great interest in each day's diversion. After remaining at the city a few days, the admiral returned to Pagoda Anchorage, and sent the "Dwarf" on to Tamsui in Formosa, in consequence of a letter from the Vice-Consul, reporting that a disturbance had occurred at the town of Twa-tu-tia, where some Chinese had attacked the house of an English merchant, and wounded a British subject. On our arrival at Tamsui, we found that the Vice-Consul had gone to Twa-tu-tia, which was about thirteen miles up the river, some distance beyond where the "Dwarf" could go, as the river became very shallow about six miles above Tamsui. As further disturbances were expected, and as there was no doctor to attend the wounded man, the doctor of our ship and myself, with a gig and crew of four armed men, started at once for Twa-tu-tia and took a Chinese sailor with us who was lent by the Custom authorities to pilot the boat. Even with his assistance, we found the last four or five miles became so shallow that we had much difficulty in getting the boat up, and we had to get out occasionally and drag her over sand banks, the tide being low.

There are several merchants' houses or hongs with tea firing establishments attached, at Twa-tu-tia, as the country people bring their tea into this place, where it has to be fired or dried again, and packed in boxes ready for sending down the river in cargo boats to be shipped in foreign vessels at Tam-sui. For the tea firing process Chinese are brought from Amoy, because they are found to be more regular at their work and reliable than those belonging to the town which is close by, and contains about 20,000 inhabitants; the boatmen belonging to the hongs are mostly from Canton. The people of the town are consequently very jealous of the Chinese from Amoy and Canton. The present quarrel originated in a dispute between the Cantonese boatmen employed by one of the hongs and the townspeople; from this cause about 100 to 200 people assembled in a mob, and attacked the hong with knives and spears. They would soon have forced an entrance and plundered it, if two English merchants from another hong, hearing of the riot, had not gallantly come to the rescue with all the Cantonese boatmen they could collect. In charging through the mob one of the merchants got severely wounded. Great damage was done to the hong. On the news arriving at Tam-sui, the Vice-Consul had immediately started with all the foreigners he could collect, about ten, principally from an English steamer that happened to be in the harbour at Tam-sui, and a few merchants, and by this prompt action had prevented further disturbance. Before starting he had applied to the Chinese steam gunboat lying in the harbour for assistance, but without success.

At a meeting which he held with the mandarins of the district afterwards, it was decided that the rioters should pay 800 dollars to repair the damage done to the hong, and 1,000 dollars as compensation to the wounded merchant, and that the two leaders of the riot should be placed in the cangue, with a suitable inscription, stating the reason of their punishment as a warning to others not to molest foreigners. The cangue consists of a large board for the criminal to place his head and hands through holes fitted for them, and is the usual punishment given in China for similar offences. Notwithstanding that the mandarins had tried and sentenced the prisoners, the punishment was not carried out; therefore, after a few days, the vice-consul requested that it should be administered as agreed on. The Chinese officials then said there would be no difficulty about the payment of the money, but that they were afraid of punishing the two leaders, as they belonged to a very powerful clan or family, who had greater power in the town than themselves, there being no regular troops in the place at that time. On this the mandarins were informed of the arrival of the gun vessel at Tam-sui, and that he and myself intended to remain at Twa-tu-tia till their sentence was put into execution. Finding we were determined in the matter, at about 9 P.M. on the second day of my arrival, soon after we had finished dinner, these two men were brought before us by a guard of Chinese soldiers armed with spears and bearing torches. It made altogether a strange and curious sight, especially when my friend quietly took a candle, put on his spectacles, and carefully read the inscription on each cangue, or large board of wood which was locked round the prisoner's neck. Everything being correct the guard and prisoners retired. Fortunately the season for firing and shipping the tea had just finished, so that all the Amoy men were sent back to Amoy, thus removing any chance of further quarrels for that season. The wound of the merchant was severe, but fortunately not dangerous; he recovered after a few weeks, and appeared quite satisfied with the compensation.

On my return to Tam-sui the Rev. Mr. M., of the

Canadian Presbyterian Church, with whom I was well acquainted, informed me that the headman of a tribe of Peppo-hoans living about sixty miles S.S.W. of Tam-sui at a place called Sin-kang, and who with many of his people had embraced Christianity, had sent to request him to visit them, as they wished to have his advice about a chapel that they wanted to build themselves. The headman also said that he was going to make a journey into the savage territory with a part of his tribe, to endeavour to purchase some land to form a new settlement for his people, whose numbers had increased very much; and that he was on friendly terms with the chief of the savage tribe that owned the valley he wished to obtain permission to settle in. He said that this chief had expressed his willingness to make the acquaintance of Mr. M. This being a very favourable opportunity for meeting some of the savages of the interior, and possibly through them of inducing the coast tribes to be kind to shipwrecked people, I gladly availed myself of Mr. M.'s offer to allow me to accompany him. Having obtained the necessary passport from the Chinese authorities, we started the day after Christmas Day with two Chinese servants, a Chinese teacher, and one coolie to carry our food, as we went on foot in light marching order. For the first twelve or fourteen miles our path lay over a table land with short dry grass and with but little cultivation. The table land lies between the Kina-yun mountain and the sea, and is about 600 feet above the water, having a very rough and slippery path up; but when on the top the air is deliciously bracing. The Kina-yun mountain is very jagged and peculiar in shape, standing out well clear of the other mountains; and being about 1720 feet high, I found it most useful in my observations for a long distance. After passing over the table land we descended into a plain or valley which was well cultivated with rice and sugar-cane. We halted for the night at a Chinese inn at the village of Sion-lek, making a walk of twenty-four miles. Our room was comparatively clean for a Chinese inn; the floor was of mud, and the walls of mud and bamboo. Unfortunately the partition between our room and the next was very thin, and we were kept awake a great part of the night by some Chinese merchants drinking, gambling and smoking opium in the next room; after which one of them, for the rest of the night, was snorting and grunting like a dyspeptic pig. We left the inn early the next morning, and after a few miles crossed over more table land till we got to the valley in which the city of Teuxham is situated, where we rested for the night, having accomplished about eighteen miles since the morning.

Teuxham is a walled city, and is the capital of the northern portion of Formosa, being the second city in the island. It is governed by a prefect, and contains about 40,000 inhabitants. Some of the shops are good, and there is a fair trade inland and also by sea, in junks from Heong-san, a village and bay on the coast about three miles off. This bay is well sheltered for junks by a sand spit, but it is too shallow for foreign vessels to lie inside. The valley round the city is well cultivated. We went to the house of the headman of the Peppo-hoan tribe, who was obliged to keep a house at Teuxham, and to reside there for a portion of the year. As the headman was in the country, his wife and brother did the honours of the house for him. They were both Christians, and were delighted to see Mr. M. The reception room was well and gaudily furnished, like that of a petty mandarin, but the sleeping rooms were very small. As soon as it was known in the neighbourhood that Mr. M. had arrived, a great number of Christians and others came to see him and to ask him to cure them of various complaints. Mr. M. had studied medicine before leaving Canada, and always took a small supply of the commoner sorts of medicine with him; his time was therefore fully taken up in attending to their wants both spiritually and bodily. When we left the house in the morning, we found that two soldiers had been stationed at the door, who said that they had orders from the prefect to attend and guard us wherever we went. Soon after leaving Teuxham our way led us through the village of Heong-san, and along the shore for some distance, and afterwards over sand hills for the greater part of the day. The glare of the sun was very painful, and greatly aggravated by the fine dust from the sand as soon as the sea breeze set in. On this coast, ophthalmia and sore eyes are very prevalent. At every village the natives came to Mr. M., who blistered freely and also used much quinine for fever and ague, which prevail to a great extent. On our return I was surprised to see how well these remedies had acted. The sore eyes are greatly caused by the people not washing the sand out carefully; in fact they looked as if they rarely treated their skins to clean water. During the afternoon we struck inland and soon got into a cultivated country again, and after a walk of eighteen miles arrived at the village of Sin-kang, where we found that our friend the headman and many of his people had come out of the village to welcome us. His wife had also arrived, having travelled by chair for a great part of the way from Teuxham.

Before becoming acquainted with Mr. M., the headman had been an opium smoker, and had so ruined his health from this vicious habit that he was not expected to live. Since that time he had been to stay with Mr. M. at Tam-sui, who had at last induced him to give up the opium; by careful treatment his health had gradually improved, and he was now excessively grateful to his English friend for all his kindness. We dismissed the Chinese guard here, as they could not go on with us into the savage territory for fear of losing their heads, there being constant warfare between the savages and Chinese. Mr. M. held service twice on Sunday, about fifty people being present. I was much struck with the great attention shown by all present to the service and the impressive manner in which Mr. M. preached, his whole heart evidently being in his subject. Among those that came with bodily ailments, was a woman afflicted with great irritation of her eyes, which was caused by the eyelashes growing inwards under the eyelid; Mr. M. having no tweezers with him, very cleverly made a pair with a knife out of a piece of bamboo, and took the lashes out, giving her relief at once.

Had this not been done she would have lost her sight altogether in a short time.

On the 30th, our Chinese servants and about thirty Peppo-hoans put on savage dresses, tied their tails up round their heads, and armed themselves with match-locks and spears, and in company with the headman we all started for the mountains. By noon we got to a sugar mill belonging to a rich Chinese planter, who entertained us at lunch very hospitably. He appeared glad to hear that the Peppo-hoans were likely to settle beyond him, because then there would be less fear of his people being molested by the savages, some of his men having been occasionally cut off by them and killed while working in the fields near the forest. His house was in a valley at the foot of the mountains, and was the most advanced Chinese settlement in that neighbourhood. After leaving him we soon got into a wild country covered with scrub and jungle; we found wild tomatoes, which are smaller than the cultivated ones and are very good to eat and have a pleasant flavour; we also found a sort of pea which is good to eat. The frontier line runs along the top of a range of mountains about 3000 feet high, and about four miles beyond the sugar mill we had stopped at. On the top of the pass we found a small Chinese watch house made of bamboo with a strong stockade round it; it contained a small guard to give notice of any inroad of the savages. The path had gradually been getting worse ever since we left the sugar mill, sometimes leading up the bed of a stream among the rocks, and at other places it became so steep that it required the use of both hands and feet to scramble up. There were few camphor trees on the Chinese side, but after passing the frontier we entered a most beautiful forest composed principally of large camphor trees that looked as if they had never been disturbed. Creepers were twining about them in the wildest profusion, and many beautiful orchids grew on the branches; we saw very few birds in the forest, but occasionally we could catch a glimpse of one or two savages gliding along among the trees and watching us, making one feel what little chance a hostile force would have against them in these woods, on account of the ease with which they could be shot down without being able to see their foe at all. The path had now disappeared, and we went along simply by the guidance of one of the Peppo-hoans. From the watch-house on the mountain we scrambled down the steep side into a valley, and then over another range of mountains about six miles from the first; and after that came to a valley running north and south for about ten miles, covered with long pampas grass on the bottom, which was growing on a good rich black soil, and possessing streams running through it. We were here met by some Peppo-hoans from their camp,

SAVAGE MAN AND WOMAN, FORMOSA.

which was on the other side of the valley. The two parties saluted each other by firing matchlocks, shouting and dancing. Shortly afterwards we came to a stream where there was an outpost of twelve savages armed with matchlocks, who after a few words with our headman allowed our party to pass on. Two of these guards were elderly women who were armed with matchlocks and long knives like the men, but wore a short petticoat besides the sort of tunic they all wear; they looked fiercer and more suspicious than the men. After deciding that we were friends this party also fired off their matchlocks in the air. Soon after passing them we came to the camp of the Peppo-hoans, which was composed of huts fenced round with a stockade of bamboo, and built on the bank of a stream. Many savages were living in the camp with one of their chiefs who spoke Chinese; some of these gave us cakes of rice and oranges as an expression of their friendship for us. Altogether in the camp, including Peppo-hoans, savages and ourselves, there were about eighty assembled. A hut was given to Mr. M. and myself and our servants, but being badly made of coarse grass did not keep out either wind or rain.

The young savages appeared frank and pleasant people, but the old ones had a very suspicious and cunning look, which, I suppose, must have been caused by the constant state of harassing warfare they live in with the Chinese and neighbouring savage tribes. Many of the young women were good-looking, and from the appearance of the savages, it was easy to see that they were closely related to the Peppo-hoan tribe we were living with. The men of this savage tribe tattoo their faces only down the centre of the forehead and chin, in a small line about one-third of an inch wide; the women have the same tattoo mark, but on the forehead only. The men wore a kind of shirt or tunic of coarse grass-cloth, which was not dyed, although some of the leading men had a kind of square patch behind of a chequered pattern on the seat of the tunic, which was also trimmed with a narrow piece of red cloth round the neck and armholes. The fighting women wore a tunic like the men, and a short petticoat or piece of grass-cloth wrapped round the waist as well. The younger women, who looked after the children and household affairs, wore a dress more resembling that of the Peppo-hoan women, consisting of loose trousers and tunic, but none of them seemed to take any pains about dressing the hair like the Peppo-hoans do. They told us that they had never seen any foreigners before; they were therefore curious about our dress and hair, remarking with pleasure that we wore no tail like the Chinese, and they seemed much struck with the light colour of our skin. In the evening, Mr. M. expounded the Gospel to a large number, in Chinese, the chief interpreting to his followers; the Peppo-hoans who had been taught sang psalms, which sounded very strange in this wild spot and strange company, with the firelight playing on the dresses and weapons of the savage-looking group around.

The next morning about thirty savages came into camp to attend the palaver of chiefs. They said the rest that had been invited could not come, as they killed a Chinese during the night and carried off his head, and that they were now engaged in holding the usual feast and orgie. After the meeting, as we wished to visit some of their villages, a large party of savages and Peppo-hoans started with us. We went along the valley towards the south for a long time without seeing any hut or village; and, at last, believing that they were taking us back towards the Chinese frontier, where, we had been told, some Chinese were at work cutting timber, it occurred to us that they intended to take advantage of their numbers to make a raid on them. We therefore told them that we wished to return to the camp, which they consented to do after some little demur.

After our return, at the persuasion of some of our friends, two of the young savages told us that they would take us to their huts. One of these men had a very pleasing expression of countenance, and appeared a man of some influence among them, and evidently took more pride in his dress and appearance than the others. We set out with these two, and also two Peppo-hoans who volunteered to go with us. Our course was to the east, up the bed of a watercourse, which led us through a precipitous gorge or cleft in the mountains that could easily have been defended by a small number of determined men against any force; the mountains on each side and in front were very high, and rose one above another till they culminated in Mount Sylvia, which is near the centre of the island, and over 12,000 feet high. This gorge suddenly opened out into a small rocky valley, where we could see huts peeping out from between the trees and large rocks, two or three together, but not built in villages. They were concealed as much as possible, so that in many cases you could not perceive that there was any house near till you were actually at it. The huts looked very neat, being built of palm leaves and bamboo. Those for the people to live in were built on the ground, with mud floors; but those to keep the grain in were built on stakes about three feet off the ground, to keep the vermin out. Small patches of ground were roughly cultivated near the huts with Indian corn; red or mountain rice was also grown on the sides of the hills, between the stumps of trees in the most careless manner. This description of rice being of an inferior quality and not requiring care and irrigation like the common rice, finds the supply of water from the constant rain in these mountains quite sufficient to bring it to perfection, and make it a very good food, though not so nice in appearance as the white rice. Some of the huts had also plum and orange trees round them. The cottage of our friendly savage was particularly neat and well built. Over the door the skulls of the wild boar, deer, and monkeys were fastened in rows; he showed us all his weapons for war and the chase, and cooking utensils which were of the most primitive description, the principal one being the still for making a rough and not very pleasant sort of spirit. As a last treat of which he appeared extremely proud, he showed us the tails of six Chinamen, tied up in a bunch, which he said had belonged to men that he had killed; each tail had a small piece of the scalp attached to it.

After leaving his hut, we continued our walk into another valley farther on, and came to a house where we heard a great noise of shouting and yelling. Our friend then told us that the orgie was being held here over the head of the unfortunate Chinaman who had been killed the night before. We therefore stopped on the opposite side of a

K

stream, and about 100 yards off the house. Our friend then crossed the stream and told those inside about our arrival; whereupon a couple of them came out in a very curious feasting dress and crossed over to us at once. At first they did not seem at all pleased at our having come there, as I suppose they thought we might tell the Chinese of the route to their house. Others soon followed, and among them the wife of a chief, to whom Mr. M. had given quinine the day before, on account of an attack of fever and ague; and she very earnestly represented the good she had received from it. Another savage bared his side to show what relief he had obtained from Mr. M.'s treatment of a skin disease of a very severe and painful description. Both of these people represented that our intentions could not be evil, or we would not have taken the trouble to help them. After hearing this, the savages became as anxious that we should go to the house and join the feast as they had previously been averse to us. We however declined their invitation with thanks, as they were all more or less excited with drink, and are very liable to get quarrelsome when in that state, like more civilized people are. They then returned to the hut where the shouting commenced again, and we returned to camp. The feasting dress consisted of a cap of deer skin, having a narrow band of scarlet cloth round it, with a cross of the same material over the top. They wore a red tunic on the body.

Mr. M. again preached the Gospel to a large number of savages and Peppo-hoans in the camp on that evening, as on the previous night.

On the 1st of January, 1873, the Peppo-hoans made their treaty with the savages, and bought the large valley from them, obtaining leave to bring in their wives and families, to build a village, and to commence cultivation at once. They also consented to a Chinese Christian teacher living with the Peppo-hoans, and said that many of them would be glad to attend his meetings as well. They appeared to have no particular religion of their own. The Chinese had long been trying to get this valley, and the savages had been gradually finding themselves less able to resist their encroachments, principally on account of the constant feuds between themselves. They had therefore at last come to the conclusion that it would be better to sell it to the Peppo-hoans, who were so nearly related to them, than to wait and probably have it taken from them by the Chinese.

The chiefs promised Mr. M. and myself to be kind to all foreigners that came into their territory, especially the subjects of Her Majesty the Queen of

England; but stated that it would be impossible for us to go on to the east coast as they were at war with the neighbouring tribes, and could not supply us with any guides in consequence. Our friends, the Peppo-hoans, having completed their business, and being anxious to return, we had no alternative but to go back with them, it being evident to the most casual observer, that it would be folly to try to cross the island in this part without the assistance of the tribes on the way. However, I trust our visit to the tribes in this vicinity will not be fruitless, in the event of any strangers being thrown into their hands. From the behaviour of these tribes to us, and the advance they have made in civilization as far as clothing, and neatness of their houses, and manners to each other are concerned, I came to the conclusion that if they were ever brought under a firm and just government, they would become a fine race of people; and could easily be reclaimed from their present barbarous practices, when the perpetual state of warfare was put an end to. From their appearance, I consider that they must be allied to the Japanese race, and probably to the Malay. A quiet and confident manner in intercourse with them, without any show of distrust whatever, appeared to influence them in the same way, even at the trying time when we unexpectedly interrupted their drunken feast. Red cloth appeared to be what they valued the most as a present. A pig is also a great luxury with them.

The night before our return, it commenced to rain and very disagreeable weather came on, and our return journey was commenced in a downpour; notwithstanding which, our party that were leaving, and those that remained in the camp with the savages, took leave of each other with shouting, dancing, and firing off all the matchlocks that would go off, the rain having damped the powder of many of them. We found our journey to Sin-kang much more painful and arduous than before, on account of the wet: the streams we had crossed over dry shod while going having now become torrents, sometimes breast deep.

Our Chinese friend at the sugar mill again entertained us, and was very glad to hear that the bargain between the Peppo-hoans and savages had been concluded satisfactorily; but he was much grieved to hear of the murder of his countryman. On leaving, Mr. M. presented him with a teapot of Dutch glazed crockery, to which he had taken a great fancy on account of the gilt on it. We arrived at Sin-kang by night, wet through and thoroughly tired.

I may as well mention here the result of the

treaty of the Peppo-hoans with the savages, and the sad end to the new settlement. Shortly after we left Sin-kang, great numbers of Peppo-hoans settled in the valley, built a village, and cultivated the land.

A Chinese Christian teacher, and also two other Chinese Christians went in with them. Everything appeared to progress very favourably, and a road was made to Sin-kang. Mr. M. visited them occasionally. However, after a time, little misunderstandings arose between the new settlers and the savages. At last the three Chinese had occasion to go to Sin-kang, and started on their journey. As they did not arrive at their destination, a search was made for them, and their bodies were at last found, not far from the frontier with the heads missing; from this mode of death it was believed that they must have been murdered by the savages. The Peppo-hoans after this became afraid for their own safety, deserted the settlement, and returned to their old home near Sin-kang.

Although the weather still continued very bad, we could not afford the time to wait till it cleared, although our friends at Sin-kang were anxious we should do so. They all appeared very sorry at our departure, especially the headman and his wife. We had much difficulty in crossing some of the rivers between Sin-kang and Teuxham, as they were very much flooded, and the current swept down with great force. At our friend's house at Teuxham, where we slept, as on our previous journey, the water was more than an inch deep in the bedroom, making it very uncomfortable. During the night, I found my bed lifting up and down, and moving in such an odd manner, that I woke up; and then, after two or three grunts, a large hog got out from underneath and went quietly out of the room. This accounted for a vigorous attack from fleas that I received when I first lay down, but no one is surprised at these companions in a Chinese house, and I therefore had not troubled myself about them much. From this place we returned to Tam-sui by a different route, which led to the east of the Kina-Yuu Mountain, and through the Chinese village of Go-kokke, where the people were building a chapel, as there were many Christians in the place. From thence we returned to Tam-sui, having hired a small boat to carry us down the river, and were heartily glad to get back again and have a good bath and sleep after the long journey. My friend Mr. M. was unfortunately laid up with fever and ague for some days after our return, from the exposure to sun and rain, and the unwholesome rooms we slept in. During my absence, a very good regatta had taken place at Tam-sui, and the community, although limited in number, showed that they were not wanting in good-fellowship and hospitality to each other and to strangers visiting the port.

On our return to Foo-Chow we luckily came in for a fête given by the director of the arsenal, who kindly asked the officers of the ship. The entertainment consisted of a lunch to sixty-four people, then dancing in the afternoon for those that wished, while the others were at liberty to examine the arsenal. It wound up with a dinner in the evening and some capital theatricals at the French theatre attached to the establishment, the performers being the French employés belonging to the arsenal. Everything went off very well, great good taste and management being shown by the host and all the officials.

On the 14th of January H.M. ship "Curlew" arrived with five shipwrecked men from the Loo-Choo Islands, who stated that they had been well fed, clothed, and kindly treated by the natives, who had even given them a feast on Christmas and New Year's Day, having found out that these were feast days with Englishmen.

While off the city of Foo-Chow, our ship's company gave a Christy Minstrel entertainment on shore in a large godown or store-house, which was fitted up as a theatre. The bachelors of the settlement gave a ball, but there were only twelve ladies present to sixty gentlemen, which is rather different to the usual proportion in England. However, the ladies performed their duty thoroughly, and every one enjoyed himself to the utmost.

CHAPTER V.

SEARCH FOR A LORCHA—CHIN-CHEW—ARRIVE AT JAPAN—ACCOMPANY THE COMMANDER-IN-CHIEF TO KOBÉ AND NAGASAKI.

ON the evening of the 31st of March information arrived that a lorcha belonging to and commanded by an Englishman had been taken possession of by the crew, and that the captain had been murdered. The crew were Chinese, from the city of Chin-Chew. It was therefore supposed that the lorcha had been taken by them to the southward, and either burnt or sold. The "Dwarf" put to sea at once to search the coast, having the Vice-Consul from Pagoda Anchorage on board to act as interpreter with the Chinese officials at the places we intended to call at in our search. We carefully examined all the bays and long inlets, and made enquiries at different towns and villages on the coast until we got to the harbour of Chin-Chew. On our way we had met H.M. ship "Elk," which was busily employed on the same errand. The city of Chin-Chew is situated on a small river, and is about nine miles from the nearest anchorage for vessels, even of the light draught of a gun-vessel. We anchored about 4 P.M. In consequence of having to leave for Amoy the next day to meet the Commander-in-Chief, I had no time to send word to the prefect of the city that I wished to see him on business, according to the usual etiquette on those occasions before paying a visit of ceremony. Soon after anchoring, the Vice-Consul, an officer of the ship, and myself started in the gig with four men and a Chinese pilot to go up the river to the city. The wind and tide being fair for the greater part of the way, we got up the river to the landing-place about dusk. We then had to walk two miles and a half through dirty suburbs and streets to the prefect's yamun. At first we were shown to the yamun of the district magistrate, but the Vice-Consul fortunately read the title over the door, and saw at once that this was not the man we wanted, and thus saved us much time in explanations. We were then shown on to the prefect's yamun, where we were kept standing outside the large gates while he was preparing to receive us. A noisy and troublesome crowd soon assembled, and became very annoying as it got dark. However, after waiting about twenty minutes the great gates were thrown open, and we were received by the prefect in his robes. On our stating the object of our search, and requesting to know if he could give us any information or assistance in the matter, he said that he had heard nothing of the lorcha, but would give orders that a diligent search for her and her crew should be made in all the coast district under his orders, and if he received any intelligence that he would let us know at once. The visit finished with tea being served and the usual civilities exchanged. When returning through the city we were followed by a large crowd, shouting at us and occasionally throwing stones, some of which struck us. Every time we turned round on the people they ran away, but soon returned again. However, at last we got back to the boat without anything very serious having occurred, and had a long pull down the river to the ship against the wind, and arrived late at night.

Chin-Chew is a very large city, and is noted for the number of stone arches in honour of Chin-Chuans who have taken high degrees at the literary examinations. It also possesses a fine large stone bridge. At daylight the next day the "Dwarf" left for Amoy, where we met the Commander-in-Chief, and from there were sent on to Hongkong to refit.

On the 31st of May, after having had a thorough overhaul of everything, and finished the necessary repairs, we left Hongkong for Yokohama. Although the S.W. monsoon usually sets in much earlier than the end of May, we experienced constant gales from the N.E., obliging us to steam close up on the China coast and to go through the Haitan straits with all yards and topmasts down on deck. We called in at Tam-sui for coal, and were then favoured with fair winds until we got to the Van Diemen's Straits, where incessant easterly gales obliged us at last to take shelter in the Inland Sea. We entered it through the Boungo channel and steamed to the treaty port of Kobé for coal. We had been detained for five days in the Van Diemen's Straits, working across under sail, backwards and forwards, the sea being too heavy for steam to be of use; and we hoped each day that the wind would change or moderate. During four days we found the current to be running at the rate of thirty miles a day to the eastward, or to windward, and therefore assisting us in keeping our position under sail, but causing a very uncomfortable and heavy sea. On the 5th day it suddenly increased to sixty-six miles, which enabled us to struggle into the Boungo channel, where we soon got calm water and fine weather. On the coast of Japan the wind is often blowing a gale, while in the Inland Sea it may be fine.

We found the Inland Sea to be quite as beautiful as it has always been represented. It is a delightful place for yachting in, there being many towns, castles and places of interest to be visited; and permission to do so could easily be obtained from the Government. I have always found the officials and people at the different ports and villages we sometimes called at, very civil and obliging. The Japanese have built several lighthouses in the Inland Sea, which render the navigation much easier, especially at night. Every part of the coast of Japan where there is any foreign traffic, is also well lighted. The lighthouses are well and economically built, and show a very good light. We met H.M. ship "Cadmus" at Kobé. After coaling we proceeded to Yokohama, where we arrived on the 25th and met the Commander-in-Chief again.

The foreign community have built fine and comfortable houses at Yokohama; those situated on the "Bluff" overlooking the town and bay are particularly pretty, with pleasant gardens around them, and plenty of trees. The camp of the Royal Marine Battalion was placed on the "Bluff," and kept in nice order; the huts carefully painted, and the little gardens attached to them giving a cheerful appearance. The officers kept a very good mess, and always showed themselves kind and hospitable to strangers; some of them being particularly obliging in showing new arrivals the various sights and temples to be visited. Their band, and pleasant afternoon parties, were a great source of enjoyment to everyone.

The drive round by the race-course is very good, and much frequented with carriages of an afternoon. The temples and tombs of the Tycoons at Yeddo are very beautiful from their carving, gilding, and quantity of valuable bronze figures. Each temple is surrounded by large trees and gardens, which are always laid out with good taste. In front of the temples there are numbers of large lanterns of stone and bronze. The temples themselves are of very simple construction, being built with enormous beams, and having high roofs of wood.

The Japanese theatre at Yeddo was a large building, with stage, pit and gallery, and the acting was going on all day. The afternoon I visited it, they were acting some historical piece; the dresses were fine and rich, and there was a great deal of fighting on the stage, the ladies in the play taking an active part. The house was well attended, but as I found the performance very monotonous I soon left the theatre. The railway takes you to Yeddo in a short time from Yokohama, as it is only eighteen miles.

The Japanese have made great progress with their Navy, having English officers to assist them. They copy the English as near as possible in dress and exercise. The corps of Marines is well drilled, and is a fine body of men; it is commanded and instructed by an officer who was formerly in the English service. There are many curios, consisting of lacquer ware and bronzes, to be got at Yokohama, but everything is much more expensive than formerly, the old lacquer being very difficult to get at all.

A slight shock of an earthquake took place whilst we were here, but Japan is very subject to them, and formerly suffered terribly from earthquakes and volcanic eruptions.

On the 8th of July, the "Dwarf" left Yokohama in company with the "Iron Duke" (the Flagship) and the "Thistle," and we arrived at Kobé on the 11th. Kobé is the foreign settlement near the Japanese town of Hiogo. It is clean and well laid out, and has much trade, its situation in the Inland Sea being so central for the richest part of the empire. The anchorage is very good in the winter, when northerly winds prevail and are consequently off the land; but in summer when the winds are from the south, a nasty sea sometimes rolls in, the Isumi Nada being about thirty miles across. Kobé is gradually taking the trade from the large city of Osaca, which is also situated on this part of the Inland Sea, about nine miles to the eastward. Osaca has a small foreign community, and the communication is kept up between the two places by small steamers that run across the bay, and also by train, which is being continued to Kioto the ancient capital of Japan, a large and beautiful city. The reason for the foreign trade increasing at Kobé, and diminishing at Osaca, is on account of the anchorage at the latter place not being so good as at the former, and there being a nasty dangerous bar across the entrance to the Osaca river. The small trading and passenger steamers are commanded and manned by Japanese, who manage them very well, but many of them are old and rickety, and sometimes blow up. Their self-confidence has assisted the Japanese in making the great strides they have made in imitating other nations. It is unfortunate that with the manners and customs of Europeans, they cannot obtain the solidity of character. At present they change everything, even to their religion, without having decided on any other to replace their former one; consequently, although Sinto-ism still continues the nominal State religion, and Buddhism that of the people, yet both are being treated with disrespect, and the party of progress appear to care very little about any religion at all. Christianity can make little progress at present on account of the great prejudice that still exists against it, which commenced in the seventeenth century, when it caused many wars and troubles in Japan.

There are some fine temples in the hills behind the town of Kobé, of which the most famous is the Temple of the Moon. It is situated about seven miles from the settlement, near the top of a mountain, and commands a most extensive view of the Inland Sea, and all the coast and country in the vicinity. It is surrounded by gardens and woods with pleasant paths. It is a favourite place of pilgrimage for the Japanese, who sometimes live here for a few days in houses attached to the temple for that purpose, and which are kept clean and comfortable by the priests. At a temple near the settlement, a white horse is kept as a sacred animal. People before starting on a sea voyage resort to this temple, and buy small plates of beans to feed the horse with, who is supposed to be able to grant favourable winds and fair weather. I could not find out how he managed for people who asked his assistance, and were going in different directions at the same time. For a present of a few copper cash, a priest will pray to the idol Dieboots to grant the request of his employer. He kneels down at the altar and lights a candle for each person requiring his good offices, sounds a gong and bows three times, each time muttering a prayer to Dieboots, accompanied with a most profound sigh. After a few minutes he blows out the candles, squats upon his haunches, and looks round smiling, as if perfectly satisfied with his performance, and very glad to get it over.

Several rivers cross the road between Kobé and Osaca. In the dry season they have but little water in them, but after heavy rains become perfect torrents, sometimes flooding the country round. The railway bridges over these rivers are therefore built on substantial iron cylinder screw piles, screwed deep into the bed; the Japanese labourers appear to work very well in driving them under the direction of English engineers.

Osaca was famous for its large castle, but it has now fallen into decay; it also possessed a government mint, which had been brought from Hongkong, and was under the management of English officials. The coinage in gold and silver was remarkably well done, and the coins were of a convenient value, especially the gold coinage, which was equal to one pound sterling or nearly so, and the silver coins about the value of four shillings, two shillings, one shilling, and smaller pieces.

It was at Osaca that William Adams landed in A.D. 1599. He was an Englishman, and had been employed as a pilot to the Dutch squadron, that had called at the neighbouring port of Saccai, also on the Inland Sea. After having had an interview with the Tycoon Iyeyas, he was taken into his service, and sent to Yeddo. Iyeyas found him such an honest and valuable man, that he raised him to the rank of a Hatto-moto (a lower order of Daimio or nobility), and gave him land producing sufficient rice to support eighty families (a man's income in Japan being reckoned by the number of cocos of rice that he possesses). William Adams married a Japanese and had a family; he lived to a good old age, and died greatly respected.

About eleven miles to the west of Kobé, there is a large castle situated on the side of a low hill overlooking the town of Akashi, and the strait of the same name which connects the two parts of the Inland Sea, namely, the Harima nada and the Isumi nada. Although the castle had been deserted for a few years, it was still in a very good state of preservation, and gave a good idea of what the feudal castles of Japan were like. The grounds all round and also inside the castle were thickly wooded with fine large pine trees. It formerly belonged to a very powerful Daimio, whose house was built in the keep, in the centre of the castle. The keep, and also the wall or rampart of the castle, was faced with stones, which were very neatly fitted into each other; watch-towers built like pagodas were placed at the angles of the walls, and over the gates. The castle was further protected by a wide moat nearly all round it. The large body of the retainers or samurai and their families lived in a town of their own, immediately outside the castle. Their houses were neatly built, many of them having little gardens attached: the roads between the houses were wide, and running at right angles to each other. This little settlement contained formerly about 1000 fighting men, who with their families would make up a population of about 5000 persons. Many of the houses were still inhabited by those who were too old or infirm to commence life again in some trade or profession, instead of subsisting on the very small allowance given them by the government since the abolition of the feudal system. This little settlement was surrounded by a mud wall, which was loopholed at the gates and where necessary for defence; it was quite separate from the commercial town, which is built on a small river and is a place of considerable junk trade, being situated at the narrowest part of the strait. The river is sufficiently deep for small boats and junks to obtain shelter in.

About A.D. 1590 and 1600, this castle belonged to the Prince of Arima, who was a Christian, and also a very powerful warrior; the greater part of the province of Arima was also Christian at that time; but eventually Christianity was entirely stamped out of this part of Japan with great cruelty. When looking over these fine castles it is impossible to help thinking of the power and the princely position held by their former owners, and admiring the patriotism that caused them to give it all up, leave their castles and followers, and retire into private life on a pecuniary compensation that they received from the government. This happened at the time that the Mikado took up the real power belonging to the crown, and the Tycoon was deposed, and retired into private life. There are hot springs in the mountains about fifteen miles from Kobé, at a place called Arima; a very small one also bubbles up about two miles from Kobé at the foot of the mountains. The tea houses in the ravines are very pretty, and much frequented, especially those that are dotted about the valley, where a beautiful waterfall comes down into a fine pool for bathing in. This place makes a pleasant afternoon's walk, as it is only about a mile and a half from the settlement. The tokaido or high road from Yeddo to Simonoseki passes through the town of Kobé, and close to Hiogo. Near the settlement it is macadamised, and kept in as good order as a high road in England, but for the rest of the way it is paved with rough stones. It is shaded by large pine trees for a great part of the distance.

On the 15th of July the "Iron Duke" (flagship), "Thistle," and "Dwarf" left Kobé for Nagasaki. We anchored in the evening at a very good harbour called Uchi-no-Uma in Soza-Sima Island, in the Inland Sea. This island is of a good size, and is very pretty, with a hilly country partly covered with trees. We were told there were deer on it, and other game. It is partially cultivated with rice and sweet potato. I found a flower like the English pink growing wild. We passed Simonoseki Straits on the 18th. It was here that Sir L. Kuper's action was fought in 1862, when he bombarded the forts in consequence of the Daimio having fired on foreign vessels when passing through the straits into the Inland Sea. The anchorage is not at all good, on account of the very strong tides and rocky irregular bottom. This must have made the battle much more dangerous to

the ships, from the great risk of getting on shore.
The Japanese junks anchor close in to the bank
near the town. The houses in the town looked
clean and neat, the telegraph hut and stations being
particularly conspicuous on account of their white
paint. The scenery in the straits is hilly, and well
cultivated, and there are fine woods in the vicinity.
After passing through the straits, we anchored at
the harbour of Furuye, in Hirado Island. In
former days the Portuguese had a settlement for
trade on this island, which at that time possessed a
large Christian population. Even now many of
the Japanese from this and the neighbouring
islands profess the Roman Catholic religion, and
visit the priests at Nagasaki, who are not allowed
to perform any religious ceremony except in the
foreign settlement there and at the other treaty
ports. The Christians on these islands appear to
have escaped the bitter persecution that their co-
religionists were subject to in the rest of the
empire. A Roman Catholic priest at Nagasaki
informed me that he believed the Japanese who
acknowledged the Roman Catholic faith numbered
nearly 20,000 in the southern part of Japan, but he
was sorry to say that a great part were Christians
only in name, it being very difficult to meet and
teach them, in consequence of the jealousy of the

PAPPENBORG ISLAND, WHERE THE CHRISTIANS WERE THROWN OVER THE CLIFF, A.D. 1636.

Page 153.

Japanese government. There are deer and pheasants on Hirado Island.

The next day we arrived at Nagasaki, and passed close to the island of Pappenborg at the entrance. This island has a steep cliff at one end of it, and formerly possessed a fort; it is covered with fine fir trees, and is very pretty. Its notoriety is caused on account of this being the place where the Christians were brought in the year 1636. They were landed and marched up to the top of the rock, where a cross was placed on the ground, which they were ordered to spit and trample on; those that refused to deny their faith were hurled over the cliff and dashed to pieces on the rocks beneath. It is related that few of these Japanese gave way, but preferred death to apostacy. Many of them were crucified near the town of Nagasaki about the same time. The Portuguese priests were also butchered by their enemies.

In the Roman Catholic chapel at Nagasaki there are two pictures describing the crucifixion of the Japanese martyrs and the murder of the European priests. The paintings are well done, but having been painted in Europe, the artist has given the Japanese Chinese dresses by mistake.

Dixon's History of Japan gives a very good account of the rise and fall of Christianity in

Japan. He shows what great power the Christians possessed at one time, and that there was no wish to persecute them at first, all sects and religions being tolerated. That afterwards when they became very numerous they behaved with great tyranny towards the Buddhists, especially in the southern provinces, where they had the upper hand. Their cruelties at last became so great that all other religions combined against them and a war of extermination commenced which eventually went against the Christians and completed their ruin.

The harbour of Nagasaki is very beautiful, and has mountains all round which come right down to the water; the numerous islands near the entrance and all the land are covered with the brightest green from the almost tropical climate and frequent rain. Many of the hills are thrown up in a very irregular manner and are evidently of volcanic origin. The native town is situated at the end of the harbour in a valley which has several streams running through it. On the sides of the hills above the town are built a great number of temples which are surrounded with graveyards. Japanese graves generally consist of a single carved stone about a foot square and two to three feet long, placed upright, with a small jar in front to contain flowers which are kept constantly renewed. These graves are always placed in pretty situations among the trees. At certain times in the year the children are sent in the evening to burn candles at the graves of their parents and relations; on these nights the whole hill side is lighted up most brilliantly. The foreign settlement is close to the harbour, clear of the town, and looks pretty and gay with the flags of the different consulates which are situated on the rising ground above the other houses. Vegetable wax is grown in the neighbourhood and is exported in large quantities. Tea is also an article of export. Although Nagasaki has a magnificent harbour and ought to be a place of great trade, yet it cannot be fully developed until good roads are made into the town from the country. The present roads are merely rough bridle paths over the hills, and can only be used by pack horses carrying very little, on account of the steep ascents. The coal mines at the island of Tako-sima give a large supply of quick burning coal, which was sold by the Japanese government for eight dollars a ton, and was exported in large quantities. The mines were managed by an English engineer, the labourers being Japanese.

It being the intention of the Commander-in-Chief to visit the Russian possessions in Tartary and Eastern Siberia, the "Iron Duke" and "Dwarf" proceeded to take as much coal on board as they could conveniently carry for such a long cruise, and also filled up with the necessary provisions. The account of this voyage will be given in the next Chapter.

CHAPTER VI.

VOYAGE TO THE RUSSIAN POSSESSIONS IN TARTARY AND EASTERN SIBERIA—THE ISLAND OF YESSO.

ON the 26th July, 1873, the "Iron Duke," "Dwarf" and "Mosquito" left Nagasaki for a cruise up the gulf of Tartary, and to visit the Russian possessions as far north as the river Amur. We first called at the island of Tsu-sima, which belongs to Japan, and lies half-way between that country and the Corea. The harbour is large and safe, and it is perfectly land-locked. The island is hilly and covered with trees. Although Tsu-sima gives the title of Prince to one of the Daimios, the inhabitants are very poor and few in number, living by the fish they catch and a little cultivation of rice, sweet potato, and hemp. The vicinity to the Corea is its chief importance, in consequence of its making a good place for the Japanese to assemble their fleet and forces at in the event of any future invasions of the Corea by them. There are some small trout in the streams, and we found the climate very pleasant. The "Mosquito" parted company here to go to Shanghai with the mails, while we continued our voyage up the sea of Japan with a fair wind, and all sail set. We passed along the coast of the Corea, which very much resembles that of Japan.

On August 1st, we anchored off the Russian settlement in Possiette Bay, which is in lat. 42° 40′, and long. 130° 45′ E. The harbour is formed by Novgorod Bay, and Expedition Bay, and is a place of great importance on account of its being situated close to the Tumen-Ula river, which forms the boundary between Russia and the Corea.

The settlement merely consisted of a few wooden huts, which were capable of holding two or three companies of soldiers. The houses were very dirty and badly built. The few natives we saw were Mantchous, ugly and grimy, and live principally by fishing. The soil appeared of a rich and dark quality, and the few potatoes that were cultivated appeared to grow very luxuriantly. It ought to become a splendid country, when there are sufficient people to cultivate it. We saw no large trees near the coast. Coal crops up near the settlement, but it is not worked beyond what the garrison requires for its own use. The Russians had a camp with about 1000 soldiers about fifteen miles farther inland. The entrance to the harbour is so narrow that it can easily be defended by a small force, especially if torpedoes were used; there are no batteries at present, although the hill where the settlement is built would command the entrance easily. We were told that this harbour rarely freezes very hard or for long. There is but little trade at present. A few small vessels call for skins, dried edible seaweed and sea slugs for the Chinese market. A gentleman who had made a trading voyage to this place in a small schooner told me that he had found spirits, dry goods, a few sheep, and fowls, to be the most profitable articles to sell or barter. There was so little live stock to be got when we were there, that even a fowl could hardly be bought at any price. Our ship's company caught a great many fish with the seine at the entrance of a small and shallow river, flowing into Expedition Bay. We found a good bed of oysters in Novgorod Bay near the settlement, with the water so shallow that we could tear them up with our hands from the boat. The Russians said there were plenty of deer and pheasants inland, but that we could not get any without dogs, as the scrub was too thick to penetrate. They also told us that tigers were numerous farther inland. The hills in the neighbourhood were low and undulating, and very different to

Japanese scenery. The climate was pleasant, but very foggy near the sea, although the fogs do not prevail far inland.

H.M. ship "Elk" joined us on the 3rd with a mail; after which we proceeded to the settlement of Vladivostok, where we arrived on the 5th, having had to grope our way along in a fog. I have often noticed on this coast, that the fog lifts a little close to the land, and as the cliffs come down pretty steep into deep water, with few outlying rocks, the navigation is not so dangerous as it otherwise would be.

Vladivostok, also called the Golden Horn, can be entered from either end of the channel called the Eastern Bosphorus, and is a deep and safe harbour, well fitted for defence and to become the principal naval station in Eastern Siberia. It is about seventy miles from Possiette Bay. For a great part of the distance, an inner channel leads by a very good passage inside the Eugénie Archipelago of islands, which form a sheltered inland sea for vessels and boats trading in the numerous bays on that part of the coast.

The Russians have already established a dockyard and building slip for small vessels, and when the plant of machinery is brought down from the dockyard of Nikolaevsk, and the change of head quarters

VLADIVOSTOK, EASTERN SIBERIA.

is thoroughly completed, it will be a very good and useful naval port. Several war vessels are stationed here, the crews of which are landed in the winter, and quartered in fine barracks made of wood. There was a garrison of about 400 soldiers who also had good barracks. I was informed that the harbour is rarely sufficiently frozen to interrupt communication entirely for any length of time, except in very severe winters. When we were in the harbour there were three Russian war vessels present, a government tug, and several steam launches belonging to the dockyard.

There was not much cultivation in the neighbourhood, although the soil appeared very fertile, and wherever vegetables had been planted in the gardens they were growing luxuriantly. When the rest of the officials come to live here from Nikolaevsk, it will soon become a much more flourishing place, as it has every capability for doing so. Some good trout and salmon peel were caught by the officers of the ships, in a stream about two miles from the settlement. We also had good deer shooting on one of the neighbouring islands. On one occasion the Russian officials kindly placed a steam launch at the disposal of the officers of our ships, who landed at Kazakavitch Island, and, forming a line across one of the long peninsulas, walked down towards the end, driving the deer before them, and they managed to shoot seven red deer; the undulating hills covered with fern and trees, much resembled the scenery of Mount Edgecombe. The ship's company caught great quantities of salmon with the seine near the end of the harbour. The church belongs to the Greek Christians, and is built of wood; the houses of the officials are also made of wood, and are kept whitewashed, which causes them to show out well from the water against the green country behind. There was only one English merchant living here, who kept a small store. He showed us every attention, and was of great service to the sportsmen.

The harbour is well capable of defence, and from its position with regard to Japan, the Corea, and China, will be a most important station in the event of any troubles in the East. Of this the Russians appear to be fully aware, by concentrating their forces here, and making it the head quarters for the Siberian or local squadron, which is under the orders of the Governor General of Eastern Siberia, and distinct from the Pacific squadron, which is under a Commander-in-chief of its own. At present the Russians keep a naval dépôt at Nagasaki in Japan, where they generally dock their ships for repair and refit. Their ships always appear to have a great quantity of men belonging to them, as far as I could judge more than either the American or French vessels of a similar size and class.

The Russian government have established schools here for the children. One morning I noticed the girls' school out for a walk on the road near the beach, while I was on board the ship. The order they marched in was most accurate; first walked the mistress with an umbrella, then all the girls in pairs, the smallest first, and tallest last, in the shape of a wedge; the girls wore large sun bonnets, but carried no umbrellas like the mistress. The effect was very comical.

WEDGE-SHAPED PROCESSION OF GIRLS.

While here, two couple of Protestants took the opportunity of getting married by the chaplain of the "Iron Duke," as there was only a Greek priest at Vladivostok. They had waited patiently for a long time, and hailed the arrival of the British flagship with joy, for putting an end to their long engagement.

From this place you can telegraph to Europe, through Japan and Shanghai, and also direct through Siberia to St. Petersburg. All places of importance on the coast are connected by the telegraph. The climate in the summer is very pleasant, although it is dreary and cold in the winter. There is a curious little kiosk on the top of a hill overlooking the harbour; the people have built a good bathing house in the harbour, to enjoy the excellent sea bathing. Altogether it bids fair to become a very pleasant as well as important place.

The "Mosquito" joined us on the 12th, when we proceeded to Wrangel Bay, and we arrived the same evening. Wrangel Bay is a beautiful land-locked harbour inside of the large bay called America Bay, and is capable of holding a large fleet; we found only a few Tartars here who lived in wretched and dirty huts. They subsisted chiefly by fishing, although at one place they were cultivating the opium poppy to a slight extent. When the poppy is sufficiently grown, the head of it is scratched all round to let the juice ooze out and harden by exposure to the air. It is then scraped off and collected. A small patch of flax was also growing close to the huts, but there appeared no other signs of cultivation. The hills, which are not high, and the country all round was covered with thick scrub, very difficult to penetrate, and long grass up to one's breast, which afforded excellent cover for deer and game. The ships' companies caught salmon and trout in the seine at the river at the end of the bay. On the 14th the Commander-in-Chief and his staff embarked on board the "Dwarf," and steamed to Nakhodka harbour, about seven miles off, where there is a small Russian military settlement consisting of two officers and fifty men. It had a government schooner moored off it. As there were no other settlers, it must have been painfully dreary work for the people, few of whom had wives; there were no roads from the settlement, except a small path kept open for bringing in wood. The houses were well built of large logs of wood, and fitted with double windows. It had formerly been a station for 200 men, but since the Russians had advanced farther south, so large a force was no longer necessary. Many of the houses were falling to decay. The harbour is too small for large vessels. The officers said tigers were numerous inland, and that one of them had carried off his dog from the settlement a short time before. In the evening we returned to our former anchorage near the rest of the squadron.

On the 15th we all left for Olga Bay, which is about 150 miles farther up the coast, and on our way ran along gaily before a fair wind, the large iron-clad and two little gun-vessels occasionally trying their rate of sailing with all possible sail set, and at other times keeping station as carefully as they would do in company with a large fleet. The "Mosquito" had been sent away with the mail when we left Wrangel Bay. Near Olga Bay the land terminated in low cliffs. Low Table Point is a capital mark to show the entrance to the harbour, and Brydone Island shows out well against the land, as it is like a cliff towards the sea, and the hills behind are covered with dark fir trees. Olga Bay contains an outer and an inner harbour. The outer one, where the squadron anchored, is quite safe. The Russian settlement is situated on the inner harbour, which is a beautiful basin with a very narrow entrance from the outer harbour, and quite concealed by the land between. We found two Russian steam corvettes at anchor in the inner harbour. The settlement seemed a busy and thriving place, the only one where we saw any farming carried on; cattle and sheep were plentiful and cheap, and we caught plenty of salmon with the seine, from nine pounds weight and under. In the streams we caught a few trout with the fly. The temperature of the sea water in August was 60° and the air 68°. On this coast the cold current of water from the Arctic comes down inshore, while the warmer water of the Japan current runs to the northward farther from the mainland, the different temperatures of the water causing constant fogs.

On the 17th we proceeded to St. Vladimir Bay, which is about forty miles to the northward, and had to grope our way along in a fog, which became so dense that we were compelled to drop an anchor at last outside of the entrance for a few hours. In the afternoon the fog cleared off for a short time, and we found the entrance of the harbour close to us, we therefore steamed inside, and anchored in South Bay. St. Vladimir Bay is a large harbour containing several bays inside of it, quite sheltered from all winds. There are several streams running into the harbour, where we saw some Tartars spearing salmon from their canoes, but the fish would not take the fly at all. The "Iron Duke" sent her seining party to haul the seine in a large freshwater lagoon, where they caught some excellent trout. The officers took the opportunity to get up a picnic at the same place, some taking their guns and some their fishing-rods with them, there being sport for all, deer, duck, snipe, and trout. After the forenoon's amusements we all mustered for lunch. As soon as the Admiral was seen to be coming from the ship to join the fun, all those that had guns fell in ready to receive him as a guard of honour. Every one was in a very odd and rough shooting costume, especially the captain of the company, who, having got his trousers wet while seining, had tied a rug round his lower limbs while the trousers were drying; but this impromptu garment did not at all conceal a remarkably good pair of calves. When the admiral arrived, the guard gave a general salute, and then fired fifteen guns, and afterwards we all pitched into lunch with great gusto. Several deer were seen, but none were shot, as the scrub was too thick to penetrate far. The trees were small and of no great value, being ordinary forest trees. The same afternoon a party from the "Dwarf" caught large quantities of salmon, rock cod, and flat fish with the seine at the entrance of a salt-water lagoon about two miles farther off. We found quantities of wild duck among the long reeds round some salt-water ponds close to the anchorage at South Bay.

On the 19th of August, we left St. Vladimir harbour at daylight, and arrived at Pallas Bay, about 420 miles to the northward, on the 21st. On our way we experienced a moderate S.E. gale which veered to the S.W., and afterwards to W.S.W., when the weather moderated and became fine. The summer gales on this coast are usually of short duration, commencing from the S.E. with thick misty rain, but as soon as the wind comes from the land the weather clears. On the above-mentioned occasion the barometer fell to 29·71, the usual height being 29·90, and the thermometer stood at 72 degrees. Pallas Bay is one of the inner bays in that magnificent large harbour called Port Imperial by the Russians, and Barracouta harbour by the English. The different bays and harbours inside are so landlocked and well concealed from each other, that vessels might easily lie in adjacent anchorages, actually within a very short distance of each other but quite out of sight. Pallas Bay is so named on account of the Russians having destroyed their frigate called the "Pallas" here, to prevent her from falling into the hands of the English during the war. None of the wreck is now visible, although the timbers still remain under water, as our seining party found to their cost in consequence of the net becoming entangled in the timber while fishing, to such an extent that it required the diver from the "Iron Duke" to assist us before we could get it clear. The country had quite altered in character as regards vegetation and scenery, since leaving St. Vladimir harbour. The low rocky hills come steep down to the water, and are densely covered with forests of fir trees, and the water is generally deep quite close up to the rocks. It was very similar to the scenery in the long inlets in Newfoundland. The climate also appeared much the same; sometimes when it was blowing hard and the weather was misty outside, there would be little wind and the weather would be comparatively fine inside the harbour where we were anchored. I have often noticed this to be the case in Newfoundland also. Another point of resemblance was in the great beauty of the reflection of the rocks and forest in the clear water during the early morning before the breeze set in; the solemn stillness of the scene being only broken by the flapping of the wings of the divers and wild duck. The fir trees near the coast do not grow so large as those farther inland, and I noticed that those that were large enough to be used for spars for vessels were constantly rotten in the centre. On enquiring about it I was informed by the Russians that this disease only affected those on the coast, that the trees inland grow to a larger size and are quite sound throughout. The Russian government will not allow any trees to be cut without their consent, the forests being crown property. There was a small military settlement at Pallas Bay, consisting of a serjeant's guard, who live in good substantial log houses. The men are employed in cutting wood for the use of the Russian war ships that call here and require it, as no coal has yet been found in the neighbourhood. The wood helps the coal out very well, although it burns quickly. On our return to this place from the north, we cut wood to use on board the "Dwarf," and found that about six tons of wood were hardly equal to one of coal; had our furnaces been fitted for burning wood, it would have answered better.

There was no attempt at cultivation or at growing even vegetables here, although vegetables grow well at Nikolaevsk which is much farther to the northward; the reason given was that the guard was constantly changed, and would never be able to reap the benefit of what they had sown or planted. The men were on rations the same as on board ship; a vessel of war calls in at regular periods to supply them with provisions. There were only two Russian women and a few children to enliven the garrison. The natives appeared of a mixed race, with something of the Esquimaux and Tartar in them; they wore a tail like the Tartars, but used their canoes like Esquimaux with double paddles. The natives were glad to sell us splendid salmon for a little biscuit, rice, or old clothes, but did not appear to care about money. There was a capital salmon river at the end of the harbour, but it had so many spent and dead fish in it that there was no fly fishing to be done.

We were all glad to find H.M. ship "Cadmus" here on our arrival with letters from England: she made a very acceptable addition to the squadron, and enlivened us all with very good theatricals one evening. On these long cruises the interchange of civilities and hospitality between the officers and men of the different ships is of the greatest value in promoting harmony and making our profession a pleasanter one than it would otherwise be, by breaking the monotony of ship life, and by cheering Jack up after a hard day's work. Some good bags of duck and snipe were made here by some of the officers.

On the 26th, we all left the harbour. When outside, the Cadmus parted company to go to Dui on the island of Sagalien for coal. The "Iron Duke" and "Dwarf" continued their journey to Castrie bay, and arrived there on the 27th, and anchored inside of Oyster Island. The "Elk" had been sent away with the mail a few days before.

Castrie Bay is not near such a good and safe harbour as those other ones on this coast that we had lately visited. Before the Russians decided on making Vladivostok their head quarters, this bay was of much greater importance than it will be in future, on account of all large vessels having to anchor here that wished to communicate with the Amur river; small ships received their pilots at this place to take them up to the town of Nikolaevsk. There is quick communication with the Amur over a short strip of land, and then by a small steamer across a lake, which cuts off a very long distance round. The telegraph comes down to the town from Nikolaevsk. The town at Castrie Bay was small; there were two gun-vessels and a small gun-boat here on our arrival belonging to the Siberian squadron.

In consequence of the Commander-in-Chief wishing to visit Nikolaevsk, and the river being too shallow for the "Iron Duke" to go up, he embarked on board the "Dwarf" with his staff at midnight on the 28th. We then weighed and made sail when outside to a moderate S.E. gale, having timed our departure so as to arrive off the outer banks about daylight. We had to proceed very cautiously on account of the heavy sea on the banks, many of which had altered since the last survey, and we had not been able to obtain a pilot for the river. At daylight the weather cleared, and we made out the land near Cape Pronge; soon after that we got safely over the outer bar, and then for the rest of the way up the river the Admiralty chart appeared nearly correct. The marks on shore were excellent and consisted of two triangles of wood painted white, which showed out most distinctly against the dark fir trees. The channel is very narrow and intricate; even for a vessel drawing only eight feet and a half of water, it was necessary to be very careful in keeping the marks exactly on to prevent grounding. The entrance of the river is about seventy-five miles from Castrie Bay, and Nikolaevsk is about eighty miles farther up the Amur. We anchored off the town at 7 o'clock in the evening. The hills on each bank are low, and covered with fir trees; the soil is rocky, but rich in the valleys.

The morning after our arrival, the Commander-in-Chief paid an official visit to the Russian Governor General Admiral Crown, who spoke English perfectly. "Droskys" were waiting for Sir Charles and the officers that accompanied him on landing, and they soon rattled us all up to the government house. The government house was built of wood, and was not very large, but was very comfortably furnished, and had a small garden around it. The streets of the town run at right angles to each other, and have pavements of wooden planks for foot passengers in order that they may be more easily kept clear of snow in the winter. The houses are made of wood, and fitted with double windows to keep the extreme cold out. Many of the houses were unoccupied, as the officials had already commenced removing to Vladivostok to prepare for the arrival of the governor general there the next year.* A great deal of the machinery from the dockyard had also been sent down. The cultivation was confined to a few kitchen gardens belonging to some of the houses; in them we saw potatoes, beans, peas, vegetable marrow, and a few other vegetables, which appeared to grow very well. All the corn and cattle for the use of the settlement is brought down the river in flat-bottomed cargo boats, which are towed by small steamers from a very fertile country in the

---

* When I left the China station at the end of 1874, the Governor-General had not changed his own residence to Vladivostok, and it was rumoured at that time that he would probably take up his residence at a town called Khabarovka, which is situated at the junction of the Amur and Oussouri rivers, a most commanding situation midway between Nikolaevsk and Vladivostok. The country in that neighbourhood is represented to be very fertile, and is famed for the exploits of the Russian captain Khabaroff against the Tartars more than 200 years ago.

interior, commencing about five hundred miles from the town, and continuing into the heart of Siberia. Mr. Atkinson's work on the Upper and Lower Amur gives a most exhaustive description of all that country.

The mail takes about sixty days to go to St. Petersburg. In the summer the journey is performed for some part of the way by steamers on the Amur, then by horses or drosky, and afterwards by rail when in the more civilized parts of Russia. In the winter, when the river is frozen hard, sledges are used instead of the steamers. For about six weeks in the spring and autumn while the river is neither frozen hard, nor yet free from ice, the communication is uncertain and irregular. The Amur Steam Navigation Company possesses small steamers well adapted for the trade on the river, which is carried up and down in flat-bottomed cargo boats; some of the steamers and boats draw only two feet of water, and some of the steamers are fitted with a wheel in the stern for the narrow parts of the rivers, which they navigate for nearly 2000 miles. The steamers were built principally in England, brought out in pieces, and put together at Nikolaevsk, where they are repaired.

The director of the Company was formerly an

officer in the Russian navy, but had retired from it when he received this appointment from the government, in consequence of his having suggested the scheme of making use of the Amur by small steamers. He had the rank of colonel in the army given him in exchange for his naval rank. He spoke English perfectly, and behaved very courteously in showing us everything we wished to see, and giving us all the information in his power.

The quantity of salmon in the river is enormous. A party of Russians hauled the seine in a small sandy bay not far from the ship, and at each haul it generally came in as full of salmon as it could hold.

The first day of our arrival, salmon was sold alongside the ship at the rate of six for one dollar, the fish weighing from six to nine pounds; afterwards, when our people were not too ready to buy, they were sold at thirty for the dollar, and the last day they came down to fifty for a dollar, the value of the dollar being about four shillings and twopence. When we left we had as much on board as would keep fresh for the ship's company, and also as much as we could salt for ourselves and the rest of the squadron at Castric Bay. There are representatives of many different tribes of natives here.

Tartars, Ghiliaks, and Ainos, who live almost entirely on fish. They appeared hardy, and are of an olive complexion; some of them wore a short tail. Skins, and everything except salmon, whether for food or household use were most expensive. We found several merchant vessels of different nations at anchor off the town.

The governor-general invited the admiral, secretary, flag-lieutenant, and myself to a lunch at the government house. It was given in the Russian style, and was very good. Several military officers were present. After lunch we all drove out into the country in droskys, where we got out and walked, and picked wild raspberries, which were very nice. The country was rough and wild, and the roads would have been fatal to the springs of ordinary carriages, although our Russian drivers rattled their shaggy horses over them famously. I can easily understand what I was told of the great fatigue of a journey across Siberia, because in a very short time the excessive jolting makes you wonder who's bones you have inside your body. After our drive we had dinner with a larger company than before, but we broke up early, and got on board by 9 P.M.

Sir Charles made several observations of the magnetic dip here, as he was in the habit of doing at every place he visited. The result of these observations will be of great value by comparing them with those obtained by himself and other scientific officers in former years.

As an example of the different routes to England that can be made use of from Nikolaevsk, I sent one letter home through Siberia, another across the United States of America, and a third by the Peninsular and Oriental and Brindisi route. The Peninsular and Oriental arrived the first, then the American one, and last of all the Siberian, which was a month longer, although it had started a few days before the others. From St. Petersburg they can telegraph to Nikolaevsk and Vladivostok, then from there to Japan, and back by China and India, thus making a complete circuit. The Russian line is the cheapest, and having no interruption, except at St. Petersburg, a telegram will reach England by this route much quicker than by the other. We had fine and pleasant weather while in the Amur, the temperature being about 70°. We remained till the 2nd of September, and were all sorry to leave when the order was given. As we fortunately had a strong N.E. wind back with us, we arrived at Castric Bay the same night, and the Commander-in-Chief changed his flag to the "Cadmus," which was waiting in the harbour to receive him, his flagship having gone to Sagalien for coal. In consequence of the "Dwarf" being very small for so many passengers, we made a tent of double canvas abaft the mizen-mast, where five of us slept in cots; another officer was accommodated in the wardroom, and the admiral had the captain's cabin. It was not only a very interesting cruise, but a very pleasant one also, notwithstanding the squeeze on board, every one being determined to make the best of it.

The day after our arrival both the ships sailed to Barracouta Harbour, and anchored in Pallas Bay, where we found the "Iron Duke" had arrived before us, having obtained her coal at Dui, in Sagalien Island. The admiral therefore changed his flag to his own ship from the "Cadmus."

There is plenty of coal to be got at Dui, but there is unfortunately only an open bay, and not good for vessels to anchor in. The weather is so unsettled and stormy that it is necessary to be prepared to put to sea on short notice, and sometimes ships take a long time to get a cargo of coal in consequence. The mines are worked by Russian convicts who have been transported for life, as this is considered one of the worst convict stations in the empire. The southern half of Sagalien contains great quantities of coal; it formerly belonged to Japan, but by recent treaties has become Russian. There are no harbours in any part of the island; the Japanese merely possessed a few fishing villages on the southern part, the climate being too severe for them to flourish in.

While we lay at Pallas Bay, an occurrence took place that might have ended very seriously. On the 8th, it was discovered that the forest behind the settlement was on fire. A party of men from one of the ships was sent to put it out before it spread far. After much trouble they thought that they had done so, but, in consequence of the deep moss, the fire continued to smoulder underneath, and at last burst out again furiously, having travelled from the original place where the trees had been cut down for firewood to the large trees around. It was a splendid sight to see the flames rush up the trees with a roar, and then the trees would come down with a crash when burnt through. Strong parties of seamen and marines were sent from our squadron, to try and prevent the fire from spreading to the Russian settlement, by cutting lanes through the trees between the fire and the settlement. But this had very little effect in stopping the progress of the fire; because, when the fire found no trees to jump to, it ran along by the thick moss, which was about two feet deep and burnt like tinder, and so beat us that way. Fortunately there was no wind at the time. We then confined our efforts to cutting the fir trees down in a circle behind the settlement, clearing them away, and then digging a trench and clearing away the moss, fir cones, and dead wood. Our blue-jackets worked hard with axes, picks, and shovels, all the 9th, during the night as well as the day. Sometimes the fire blazed up so high, and the sparks flew so far, that it seemed impossible to save the houses. The Russian soldiers had sent off their valuables, and were ready to embark themselves in the flagship's boats if necessary. It continued burning all the 10th, and kept our people still hard at it, who found it no easy work to clear the ground, and cut through the roots of the trees; and caused many of us to come to the conclusion that it must be pretty tough work for emigrants who settle in the backwoods and clear their land, and that it would take a long time to clear away sufficient to make a living. On the night of the 10th, a light breeze sprung up, which sent the sparks so thickly over the harbour, that the "Iron Duke" had to change her anchorage, to keep clear of them for fear of catching fire; the sparks flew as high as the masts, and there was danger of their lodging in the sails and burning them. The fire by this time had burnt down to our trench, which the officers and men strove hard to keep it from crossing, by beating it out and throwing water on it. Many of them got burnt and bruised from falling trees, although none were seriously hurt; but it was warm work. Although the trees had been cut down for some distance in front of the trench to prevent us from being scorched by the heat, yet nothing could have saved the houses, had not the wind fortunately changed when we were commencing to despair and feel that, although everything had been done that could be, our men were getting used up by fatigue and heat, and the flames were still gaining on us. Towards morning a breeze sprang up from the S.E. accompanied with thick drizzly weather, which eventually became a gale with heavy rain. By the wind coming from this direction, the fire was driven on to the part of the forest that had been already burnt, and soon went down, leaving the settlement quite safe.

The "Cadmus" had left us here to carry a mail to Japan : and on the 11th, after finding everything was safe on shore as regarded the fire, the "Iron Duke" and "Dwarf" left for Hakodaté, in the island of Yesso, belonging to Japan. When outside we got separated from the flagship in a gale, and afterwards, on rejoining her, were directed to make the best of our way to save the coal as much as possible, the weather having become very unsettled as the season was well advanced, and the autumn gales had set in early on this coast. When off the West Coast of Yesso, we encountered a heavy gale from the S.W. We were then sailing along near the shore in the large bay called Iskarri, of which we had no good chart on board. We noticed that there were several Japanese junks in a bay that was not marked in our chart, and that looked inviting and well sheltered. Finding the wind and sea increasing so much that we could not weather Cape Tomamoy, the most westerly cape in Yesso, even by using steam, we ran cautiously into the bay and anchored near the junks in seven fathoms water.

The next day it blew very hard, we therefore amused ourselves by making a survey of the bay, as it appeared a very good one and free from rocks. We found the western point near the village to be in lat. 43° 17′ 45″ N. and long. 140° 35′ 15″ E., and about ten miles from Cape Tomamoy. The best anchorage was in from five to eleven fathoms of water. The only winds that it is open to are those from N.N.W. to N.E., but the natives told us these rarely prevail, and seldom blow hard; indeed the position of the houses, which are built close down to the water, showed us that a very heavy sea could not roll in often, or they would be washed away. The country round was mountainous, and the cliffs bold and rugged. The villages looked very pretty nestling in under them, the high roofs of the temples giving a very quaint appearance to the villages.

Two Japanese Bhuddist priests came on board with a large number of attendants to pay their respects and make enquiries about the reason of our visit. They were very polite, and brought us a present of sweet biscuits and flowers. We had tea and wine in the cabin, and they seemed much pleased to see the ship, the guns, and other things that they said they had not seen before. They called their village Maro-Yama. Numbers of the natives came on board to see the ship. Some of them were Japanese, but the greater part were Inos, a race that inhabits Yesso, the north of Niphon and Sagalien, and are treated with great contempt by the Japanese. They had a great quantity of thick black hair, and a dull and heavy expression of countenance. The Japanese are mostly the shopkeepers here, and more wealthy than the Inos, who live by fishing and cultivating just sufficient for their immediate wants. The Japanese have credit for honesty, but on this occasion we missed several things when our visitors left—a pair of double-glasses belonging to one officer, and soap out of some of the cabins, for which, I suppose, the Inos are responsible, as they have no character to lose, and would certainly be all the better for a little soap. Although our friends, the priests, said that they would try to recover the glasses, they did not succeed in doing so, but told us at last that they were afraid the thief knew that by their law he was liable to lose his head for his offence, and had therefore concealed or made away with the glasses. There is a large valley at the end of the bay between the hills, with a stream running through it, where there is a great quantity of trout. The country inland was wild and uncultivated, and it was very difficult to penetrate the thick woods of scrub and small forest trees. The population was very small, and evidently did not inhabit much beyond the coast line.

On the 17th we put to sea, and tried to get round Cape Tomamoy as the wind had hauled round more from the W.N.W.; but when well outside of the bay it blew so hard that it was not possible to struggle round it, as the sea was very heavy, and made our screws come out of water at every dive; we therefore wore round and ran back to our snug little anchorage again. However, on the following day the wind moderated, and we got clear away and arrived at Hakodaté all safe, where we found the flagship at anchor, having arrived the day before. She had been compelled to lay-to at sea during the gale that we had quietly ridden out at anchor in our little bay. The harbour of Hakodaté is situated on the south side of the island of Yesso, and on the north of the Straits of Tsugar. It is a very safe harbour, and when the island of Yesso is more colonised by the Japanese, and opened out, will probably become a place of considerable importance, in consequence of the quantity of coal and sulphur mines in the island. The trade at present is conducted principally by junks that bring rice from China or other parts of Japan, and take back dried seaweed in return. The mails are carried to Yokohama by a steamer once a month; there is also a Japanese post that runs regularly by land through the island of Niphon.

The country is of volcanic formation, the mountains running up into peaks, those above the town of Hakodaté bearing some resemblance to Gibraltar, on account of their being connected with Yesso by a low sand spit. It was at this place that the naval action was fought between the forces of the Mikado and the Tycoon, which decided the fate of the latter, who surrendered the executive power into the hands of the Mikado, and was afterwards allowed to retire into private life. It is said that many of his followers were dissatisfied at his not performing the "Hari-kari," and disembowelling himself according to the custom of high-minded Japanese noblemen when they are defeated. The wreck of one of the Tycoon's steamers was still lying on the beach when we were at Hakodaté. The harbour is protected by a fort at the entrance; the ruins of another fort still remain on the sandy spit connecting the town with the island of Yesso. The foreign society is very limited, consisting principally of the officials belonging to the different consulates, and in the summer several of the residents of Yokohama come here for the benefit of their health during the hot weather, the climate being pleasant in the summer, but very cold and dreary in the winter, with much snow and stormy weather.

The volcano and sulphur springs about twenty-two miles inland are well worth a visit on account of the pretty scenery on the road, which winds between the hills and round the borders of a lake. Here and there you pass through ravines which are overhung with precipitous rocks and crowned with forest trees. Some American gentlemen have established a farm about half-way out, at the expense of the Japanese government, to endeavour to encourage cultivation among the people. They have also made a fine road, and planted a Japanese colony about eighty miles inland from Hakodaté. Unfortunately the colonists were brought from the south of Japan where the climate is very different, and were now anxious to return, as they could find no market for their produce so far from any civilized place, and the allowance of rice the government had allowed them for three years would soon terminate. Yesso produces the usual fruits and plants of a temperate climate; the hop grows most luxuriantly in the hedges: I also noticed grapes growing wild, but they were hardly fit to eat. The produce from the country is brought in on pack horses, which follow each other in single file in a long string, and keep to one little track in the road, which is wide enough for three carriages abreast. Yesso will probably prove to be a very valuable island when it is more thoroughly examined, because, from what is now known of it, it is rich in coal, sulphur and minerals; the forests in the interior must also become very valuable in a few years. A little beyond the farm there is a village with several large tea houses for the use of travellers and visitors who may be staying in the neighbourhood to enjoy the scenery and the trout fishing. The houses in the town and country are built in the Japanese style, but are very low on account of the violent winds: the wooden roofs are loaded with large stones to prevent the wind tearing the shingles off.

On the 27th September the squadron, consisting of the "Iron Duke," "Frolic," "Thistle" and "Dwarf," left Hakodaté for the harbour of Nambu, which is situated on the east coast of the island of Niphon. While passing through the straits of Tsugar we found the current running very strongly to the eastward, and causing a regular tide race, and a nasty chopping sea which must be very dangerous in stormy weather. The current always runs in the same direction in these straits on account of the water being pent up in the sea of Japan, and forcing its way out to the ocean by this channel.

On the 29th we arrived at Nambu, which is a large and safe harbour with a narrow entrance and hills all round it. It is very pretty to look at on entering the harbour, to see the hills and mountains rising one above the other in succession, with beautiful valleys between; the country well cultivated at the base of the hills and in the valleys, and with many neat little villages dotted about; the rest of the hills being clad with pine

trees or scrub to the top, and looking beautifully
green and fresh. There was only a small trade by
junks. The people seemed poor, but very comfortable and happy, especially the children, who always
seem happy in Japan, as they are not tortured by
many garments, and can roll about and play on the
mat floors without any fear of breaking furniture
or doing mischief. We found plenty of small
chestnuts on the hills : the chief articles of cultivation were rice, sweet potatoes, and ground-nuts, also
flax, and bird-seed. There were great quantities
of pheasants here, and several good bags were
made. Although the people sold us deer's horns
very cheap, yet we saw no deer near Nambu, so I
suppose they are brought in from the interior of
the island.

On the 2nd of October, the squadron left for
Yokohama. The day after leaving, the barometer
began to fall very suddenly from 29·93 at 4 A.M. to
29·47 at 3 P.M., the weather looking dirty and unsettled. The wind shifted from N.E. by E. to East,
and freshened up to a gale ; after which it still
continued to change to S.E., South, S.W., and
West, when it blew very hard for a few hours. It
then changed to N.W., and the barometer began to
rise, after which it settled down to a steady and
moderate gale from the northward. On account of

the constant and rapid changes of wind, the sea became very confused, running into pinnacles and causing much water to fall on board of us. The "Dwarf" stuck by the flagship and we got into Yokohama together: the other two gun-vessels arrived a few hours after. All the vessels proved themselves to be excellent sea-boats, even in the very irregular sea we had experienced.

The cruise to the Russian possessions during the summer restored our ship's company to a fine state of health, after having been much debilitated by the previous two summers in China.

CHAPTER VII.

ASCENT OF FUSI-YAMA MOUNTAIN IN JAPAN.

On the 6th of October, 1873, the captain of the flagship, admiral's secretary and myself, having obtained the necessary leave of absence from the Commander-in-Chief, started from Yokohama for a cruise inland, to see the country and refresh ourselves after our late sea voyage.

Through the kindness of one of the officers of the Royal Marines, who was stationed in the camp, we had managed to engage the services of a Japanese called "Gong," who was to act as interpreter, pay our bills, procure us good quarters and provisions, and to see that we were not cheated by anyone besides himself. He turned out to be a very useful and civil man, always ready to make the best of everything, and kept our expenses down to a very reasonable amount. We had another Japanese called "Shouski," who acted as cook, packed up our luggage and bedding, secured it on the packhorse, and then walked off in charge of everything to our next halting place. We took a packhorse, instead of coolies, as it can carry sufficient for three people, and is consequently less expensive than coolies would be. The cook proved to be a capital man, both professionally and also in managing the horse and luggage, so that we never suffered any inconvenience by his being late. He certainly earned his pay well.

We had decided to go first to the village of Mi-a-nosta, which is situated in the mountains a little more than forty miles from Yokohama. There was a carriage road for thirty-three miles of the journey: we therefore hired a wagonette to take us as far as the town of Odawarra, where the road ends, and from that place we walked up the mountain path to Mi-a-nosta, which was about eight miles farther on, and put up at a large and well kept tea house in the village. The Mikado occasionally made use of this tea house in the summer, in order to enjoy the cooler climate of the mountains, and to take advantage of the hot sulphur baths belonging to the house, which are kept constantly supplied with water running through them from mineral springs. As his rooms were vacant when we arrived, they were given to us to use, and we found them very comfortable and enjoyable; the verandah overlooked a pretty Japanese garden, which had ponds stocked with gold fish, and possessed a lovely view down the valley. There are several other tea houses in the neighbourhood, which are much frequented by Japanese and foreigners for the use of the springs; the former consider the water to be a cure for nearly all diseases that man is subject to, especially diseases in the skin and feet that are very prevalent. The gardens of the houses are very quaint with their stunted trees, which are grown into various shapes, of animals, birds, and dragons; also their fish-ponds with curious little miniature bridges over them, and carved figures of houses, castles, men and animals, scattered about the little rockeries. It was a great amusement to feed the gold fish in the morning in this delicious climate, before the sun got high. Those that do not care for a hot bath can take a cold one in the garden, under a small waterfall, made by the water from a stream being conducted along a large pipe about ten feet from the ground, and emptying itself into one of the ponds. As I did not like the publicity of the garden for my bath, I managed to get a tub of cold water in the bath-room after some little trouble and explanation, as the Japanese were not able to understand how any-one can use cold water when they can get hot.

The floors of the tea houses are entirely covered with mats about an inch thick, and it is customary to take off your boots before entering the rooms, for fear of damaging the mats. The beds consist of mattresses spread on the floor, and covered with cotton quilts, instead of blankets, and are clean and comfortable. Mi-a-nosta is about 1,160 feet above the sea, and the road leading up to it from Odawarra is very pretty, as it winds between the hills and is shaded by trees; the country is well cultivated with rice wherever the nature of the ground admits of it. There are many temples scattered about, which usually have an avenue of old fir trees leading up to them, and are always situated in very pretty places, which shows the good taste of the Japanese in taking advantage of the beautiful scenery to the fullest extent.

After we had been here a few days and had visited many pretty places in the neighbourhood and the different baths and waterfalls, we arranged to leave the heaviest portion of our luggage in charge of the keeper of the tea house, and to start on a journey to the mountain of Fusi-yama, which is the sacred mountain of Japan and one of the highest. Fusi-yama is held in such great respect by the Japanese, that a picture of it is represented on nearly all their crockery, cabinets, and other lacquered ware.

At 10 A.M. on the 9th, we left the village of Mi-a-nosta on foot accompanied by our faithful attendant Mr. Gong, the cook having started a little earlier with the baggage on the packhorse.

We had to cross a range of mountains about 2,000 feet higher than Mi-a-nosta, and then to descend into a beautiful plain or valley which was rich and well cultivated and about 1,700 feet below the top of the range we had just crossed. We put up for the night at a very nice tea house at a village called Go-tem-bah which was about fourteen miles from Mi-a-nosta, making a very pleasant walk. Here we got an upstairs room, which we found a great luxury, in consequence of its being quiet and well clear of Japanese travellers, and the cooking arrangements, which are all carried on in the large public room downstairs. We found the Japanese very primitive and simple in their habits. At this tea house, men, women, and children washed in a large tub of hot water in the evening in the public guest room without any idea that there was any indecency in the performance; after the tubbing operation, the old women and little girls shampooed the arms and legs of their guests. They seemed very much surprised that we objected to perform our ablutions in public with them; but when they at last understood that we wished to tub in private, after much laughing and joking among themselves, they gave us another room for that purpose. The walls of the bath houses that we had passed in the mountains were made of an open lattice work, which did not prevent any one that was passing from seeing men, women and children splashing and paddling about together in nature's full dress; not even the doors were fastened.

At the tea house, the wife of the landlord carried the keys and superintended the rooms and meals of the guests, and made out the bills, while the old mother took charge of the shampooing department; the landlord apparently taking matters very easily. All the married women blacked their teeth, which made them appear hideous. They have a very high character for virtue after marriage, and the law is very severe against any faithless spouse. Everyone appeared cheerful, industrious and full of fun, always laughing and joking with each other.

The following day we walked to the village of Shi-bash-ere, which is situated near the foot of the mountain of Fusi-yama. It was a very pleasant walk of about seven miles and a half through a fertile country with well cultivated fields; the villages and farm-houses were generally surrounded with clumps of bamboo, parsamum, and orange trees. It took us nearly all the afternoon at Shi-bash-ere to arrange for guides and coolies to

carry our baggage and wood for making a fire up
the mountain the next morning; as all the rest
houses on the way were closed in consequence of
the lateness of the season, we had to arrange about
obtaining permission to use one, and to get the

JAPANESE MOUNTAIN COOLIE.

key. Although we only took a blanket apiece and
sufficient food and wood for us and the coolies, we
had to engage nine of them, as each man carries a
very little in consequence of the steepness of the
mountain. We managed to engage the rest house
called No. 7, which is about 10,000 feet above the
water, and we intended to sleep there during the

night. There are a great number of these houses at regular intervals all the way up the mountain for pilgrims to make use of. They consist of one room made of lava or stone and have a door but no window. In the summer they are kept open, but are closed about September and the door is covered outside with large stones to preserve it from the storms during the winter. We found the tea house in this village not nearly so good as the one at Go-tem-bah. Our room was not nearly so comfortable and it was almost impossible to get to sleep on account of the annoyance occasioned by smells and fleas. The landlord was also very extortionate in his charges notwithstanding the remonstrances of the faithful "Gong."

We were glad to leave at 8 A.M. the next morning and commence the ascent, although the weather had unfortunately changed and become very cold, with showers of sleet and rain, which rather bothered our barometric observations, and made them more difficult to calculate and less reliable. Including the guide, interpreter, cook, and coolies, our little army mustered fifteen altogether. The Japanese had sagaciously put on their straw rain coats, which made them look as if they were covered with a thatch like a house. The landlord told us we were too late to manage the ascent, on account of the snow on the mountain, but as it was a case of now or never, and we had decided to do it if possible, away we went.

The mountain forms a perfect cone, and for the first 6,500 feet is clothed with a dense forest of trees, which change their species and get smaller in size as you ascend. While following the paths through the forest we were tolerably sheltered from the gale, and enjoyed the climbing, and laughed at an occasional slip or fall and the comical appearance of our followers, and the long face that Mr. Gong put on at the journey before us. We took our lunch at a house called the "Wood-Cutter's Lodge," which is situated in the forest, and during the summer is kept like a tea house to supply food and fire to pilgrims; but when we passed no one was living there, and it was closed.

The trees ceased quite suddenly, and gave place to a belt of heather and moss, which in turn was succeeded by ashes and scoria for nearly 6,000 feet of the last part of the mountain. Directly we got clear of the trees, we found that the wind was blowing a gale, the violent gusts coming at one time round one side of the mountain and at another round the opposite side, making it very difficult to keep our footing in the loose cinders, even with the help of a good bamboo staff. We passed many rest

houses or huts on the way, which were all built
exactly alike, and it appeared as if we should never
get to the one we wanted. At last, about dusk, we
arrived at No. 7, all of us being pretty well done
up with fatigue, wet, and cold. After clearing the
large stones away from the door, we managed to
get it open and crawl inside, and obtain shelter
from the snow that was now coming down fast.
This hut was about 10,200 feet above the sea. It
was some time before we could get our fire to light
in consequence of the rascally tea house keeper
having supplied us with green wood instead of dry;
unfortunately we had trusted all the details to him
and Mr. Gong without sufficiently examining the
articles ourselves. Our coolies made another fire
for themselves at the other end of the hut, and the
place became in a short time so full of smoke that
it caused the water to run from our eyes, and made
us sneeze violently. It became so disagreeable at
last that we were compelled to open our door to let
the smoke out, to prevent being smothered, although
we kept our faces as low on the ground as possible
to get the purest air. As soon as the door was
opened the wind and sleet blew in, and, to add to our
discomfort, the heat of the fires caused the snow on
the roof to melt and leak through, falling drop after
drop on our faces when we tried to get a snooze.

As for our poor coolies, who had come up very lightly clad, they were squatting as close round their fire as possible, shivering, smoking, talking, and eating rice during the night as greedily as if they had not had a meal for a week.

The next morning we were not sorry to see the day break, and to get some breakfast, and stretch our limbs to get the blood into circulation again. About 7 A.M. the snow ceased, and the clouds broke, giving us most lovely glimpses of the mountains, land, and sea beneath us. A glorious sight and not easily forgotten! The furious gale whirled the clouds in eddies beneath us, chased them round the mountain peaks, rent them in pieces, and hurled them in all directions. The sun tried to break through for a few minutes, but soon gave up the attempt in despair, and the snow-storm came on again as bad as ever.

As soon as we were ready we started for the top of the mountain, which took us about two hours, in consequence of the snow making it very difficult to climb up, and causing us to slip back incessantly. All our coolies came with us, as it would be considered a meritorious action for them to make their pilgrimage in such trying weather. As near as we could judge, we considered the top of the cone to be about 12,600 feet above the sea by our mountain barometer. This height agrees pretty well with that given in the Admiralty charts, although I have read some accounts that call the mountain 14,000 feet high. After examining the crater at the top of the cone, and having paid our respects to the little joss-house dedicated to Buddha, we commenced to descend as soon as possible on account of the snow-storm, which now came on very thick; the wind was so strong that we found it difficult to keep our footing, and prevented us from examining the crater as much as we should otherwise have done. We therefore hastened down to the rest house, where we arrived in a very short time by sliding through the snow. We collected our things here as quickly as possible, and then took a different route down the mountain, where the ashes were quite small and loose, making the descent very rapidly in consequence, although it would be very difficult to ascend by that way. We soon got our blood into circulation, and recovered our spirits by the exhilarating effect of the rapid motion of going down—slipping, sliding, and jumping, with an occasional tumble and roll down the soft snow. By the time we got to the forest the storm abated, and by the time we got to the village of Shibash-ere the weather cleared up altogether. Finding we had time to push on to our former good quarters at Go-tem-bah, instead of passing another uncomfortable night at Shi-bash-ere, we settled up with the landlord, and, much to his disgust, started on our journey, arriving at Go-tem-bah by night, where we had a good tub and supper, and chatted and laughed over our troubles of the last thirty-six hours. When we lay down we were so tired that we slept for twelve hours without waking. On our return journey we checked the barometric observations we had previously made of the different altitudes, and as our descent was so quickly accomplished I do not think the calculations can be far out.

The earliest account of Fusi-yama that I have met with is that of one of the Jesuits, who states that it was an active volcano in A.D. 1600. That in 1707 an eruption took place, which did great damage to the country, and lasted during fifteen days. An earthquake also took place in the island of Niphon at the same time. The Japanese have a tradition that the mountain was thrown up in a single night, and in one of their picture books about the mountain there is a humorous representation of the astonishment of the natives who first discovered the mountain when they woke up in the morning. They have also another picture vividly representing the discomfort occasioned to the house and family of the Japanese gentleman who was living at the place where the volcano burst forth; the manner in which they are all being scattered was most amusing and well drawn. Women are allowed to make a pilgrimage to and ascend Fusi-yama once in sixty years; the last occasion was 1860.

The slopes of Fusi-yama, and the neighbouring hills and plains, are covered with a rich black soil, which is very similar to that near Mount Vesuvius, and from the luxuriant manner in which the wild grapes grew all about, I believe that the vine might be brought to as high a state of cultivation as in Europe, the climate being very much like that of Italy. The grapes that are brought into Yokohama for sale are fine, but require more cultivation before they can become valuable for making wine; however, it shows what could be done if skilled labour were employed from the vineyards of Europe, and the best varieties of vine imported. There were many miles of beautiful rich plain in the neighbourhood of Fusi-yama mountain, quite uncultivated and covered with long grass, a few farms being scattered about here and there.

The morning after our return from the mountain was perfectly lovely, with a bright sun and crisp autumnal feeling in the air, and everything appeared fresh and nice after the storm. We had a good breakfast, and then walked across the valley to the Pass of Otone, which we quietly ascended, and thought nothing of 1700 feet after what we had done two days before. When we got to the top of the Pass, we rested and enjoyed the scene of the large valley beneath us, with its small river flowing through it and villages dotted about, which were surrounded by clumps of bamboo and orange trees; right in front of us the lofty cone of Fusi-yama reared his head up above the clouds, covered with his winter's coat of snow, which shone dazzlingly white in the bright sunshine. In the evening we arrived at Mi-a-nosta again, and took up our former rooms. Several other Europeans had arrived at the tea house during our absence, among whom was a gentleman belonging to the English consulate, who became a very pleasant companion during some of our rambles while here.

We made an excursion on one day to a village called Haconé, which was about seven miles off, across the mountains, and situated on a lake of the same name. Haconé is famous for the beauty of its scenery, and a long avenue of fine cedar fir trees along the borders of the lake. No description can do justice to the beauty of the scene across the lake, of which the Fusi-yama mountain forms the principal object. On our way to Haconé we stopped at a tea house, which was situated on the top of the range of mountains, to examine the hot springs which bubble up close to it. These springs appeared very strongly impregnated with sulphur and carbonic acid, much stronger than those at Mi-a-nosta. There were several baths attached to the tea house, and also to some other houses which were crowded with Japanese taking advantage of the water, the springs being considered very beneficial for the cure of elephantiasis, and all diseases in the legs and feet. The climate at this place was much cooler than at Mi-a-nosta, and the owner of the tea house was sanguine in hoping that by making his establishment comfortable for foreigners, many of them would resort to it in the summer. The ancient barrier between the East and West of Niphon crosses the road near Haconé. It consists of a rampart and barrier gate with a guard house, but it has now fallen into disuse. We returned to Mi-a-nosta by a different route; for a portion of the way along the broad high road which runs from Yeddo to Miako, and is paved with rough stones like the old Roman roads; very durable but excessively jolting and fatiguing.

On the 16th we left Mi-a-nosta, with its beautiful valleys and waterfalls, and walked to the town of

Odawarra, where we had lunch, and examined the old castle. This castle is now in ruins, but must have been a very fine one formerly, as it covers a very large extent of ground, and possesses three lines of fortifications and moats, the inner one forming the keep for the residence of the Daimio and his family. The houses are gone, but the massive ramparts still remain nearly perfect. A small guard live inside the walls in a few Japanese houses. It must have been very strong in the days of bows and arrows, but it would require an army to defend it, and there are so many hills in the vicinity that overlook the walls that it would be of no use against modern artillery. The woods outside the walls, in the grounds belonging to the castle, are very beautiful and come close up to the moat; they would afford good cover for any attacking force, and show that the castle could not have been besieged for many years. The manner in which the trees have been allowed to grow both inside and outside of the castles in Japan, shows that theirs is no vain boast of having suffered from no wars for 200 years previous to their recent intercourse with foreigners; in fact, ever since they massacred the Christians, and during the time they shut themselves up from the rest of the world. Outside the castle gate is a well laid out town, for the retainers of the lord of the castle. The commercial town of Odawarra is of great extent, and does a good trade in fish, as it is situated on the large bay of the same name, where fish is plentiful. Young shark from three to five feet long seemed the most favourite sort, and we constantly met horses and mules carrying them into the country, one strapped on each side of the animal's back.

From Odawarra we walked on to the village of Mazawa, about six miles farther, where we hired gin-rick-shas (small two-wheeled carriages drawn by one man, or if necessary two men, tandem fashion), as we wished to push on quickly, and the country was level. The gin-rick-shas are very convenient and have not long been introduced into Japan; the Japanese usual mode of conveyance being in a cango or kind of couch carried under a pole by two men, which is very convenient for short and supple-legged Japanese men and women, but very uncomfortable for foreigners. The cango has still to be used on the bridle paths and over the mountains, where the gin-rick-sha cannot travel. In the present case we had two men to each of our gin-rick-shas, who rattled us along famously over the rough road, and jolted us till we felt that our bones would soon wear holes in our skins; we accomplished fifteen miles in three hours, and put up at the town of Fugi-sawa for the night. Our road ran through a level country, with a few low hills occasionally.

From Fugi-sawa we walked the next morning across the rice-fields to see the great bronze idol of Dieboots, which is considered one of the most wonderful productions of Japan; although there is a larger one in bronze at Narah, near the city of Quioto, but the latter is not so well finished. In ancient times there was a large temple near Dieboots, but it has entirely disappeared, except a few stones that mark the places where the columns rested. The bronze idol is still quite perfect, and is taken care of by a few priests who live close to it and sell pictures and photographs of it, and also English beer to thirsty foreigners. The bronze was cast in pieces, put together afterwards, and beautifully joined. It measured forty-two feet in height from the stone platform to the top of the head; the circumference was ninety-eight feet. An avenue of trees leads up to it, and it is surrounded by low hills, which are covered with foliage and cut up by ravines in all directions. When the idol was made, the capital of Japan was situated in this neighbourhood, and called Kamakura, but was destroyed by war in A.D. 1332. At that time there were beautiful temples in the neighbourhood, many of which were also destroyed. Kama-kura was raised to the rank of the capital city by Yoritomo in 1185, when he became the Tycoon, or Commander-in-Chief, and seized the real power of the empire out of the hands of the Mikado. It then numbered 200,000 inhabitants, but when we passed through there was little remaining to show that a large city had ever existed, and at present there are hardly 500 people where it stood.

Two or three miles from the idol we passed a large temple, which was kept in a good state of preservation and appeared to be held in great esteem, judging by the number of pilgrims visiting it. It was situated in a fertile plain near the site of the old city, and had a large number of priests belonging to it; the grounds were laid out with fishponds having stone bridges over them, and planted with shrubs and flowers. A fine avenue of trees led up to the entrance, and stalls were erected on each side of the road to accommodate the pilgrims, all sorts of food and fish being sold at them, and also pictures of Buddha and maps of the country, books, and trinkets.

It was not far from this place that Mr. Richardson, an English merchant, was cut down and killed, while passing along the Tokaido or high road on horseback, with his wife and one or two friends. He was set upon by the followers of the Prince of Satsuma, for not getting off the road while their lord passed on his way to Yeddo. The lady and friends escaped to Yokohama by hard riding. Mr. Richardson had made his fortune in China, and had merely come on a visit to Japan before his return home.

In consequence of the Japanese Government being either unable or unwilling to punish the murderers, the British squadron under the command of Sir L. Kuper bombarded the forts at Kagosima, the capital of Prince Satsuma, in 1862, as no satisfaction could be obtained by milder measures, and foreigners had so constantly been insulted and ill-used that it was necessary to put an end to it with the strong hand.

By the old law of Japan, when a nobleman of high rank passed along the road with his followers, who sometimes numbered as many as 200 people, everyone of lower rank had to get out of the way, and in the event of their failing to do so, were badly treated by the retainers. When Daimios of high rank were required at Yeddo, the route they had to take was notified to them beforehand by an officer of the court, in order to prevent two of them meeting on the same road and causing a disturbance, and probably a fight. The lower orders had to kneel when a Daimio passed; all points of etiquette were rigidly enforced in the feudal times.

Kama-kura must have been a good situation for the capital, as it was close to the Gulf of Suruga, and tolerably central in position with regard to the rest of the island, and possessed a fine fertile country around it. From Kama-kura we passed over a very pretty country with low hills, which had the appearance of having been broken up by a series of earthquakes. The hills were covered with trees and bushes, but the valleys were well cultivated with rice, sugar-cane, sweet potatoe, and flax. The farm-houses were very neat-looking, situated among orange and parsamum trees. We lunched at the fishing village of Cana-wa, and arrived at Yokohama in the evening, having walked about nineteen miles since leaving the idol of Dieboots.

In consequence of the number of war-ships of different nations that frequent Yokohama, and the many temptations for the seamen while on leave, there being no place where they can go to for a quiet dinner and bed, several of the residents started a kind of home for them to use when on shore. This home was commenced when we were at Yokohama on this occasion, and, I believe, has proved a great success. It was started on temperance principles; the seamen and marines of any nation could go there and obtain their meals and beds at a very reasonable rate. This was all the more valuable to them at Yokohama, because the anchorage is so exposed in bad weather that it is sometimes impossible for boats to communicate with the ships, and they were therefore often compelled to sleep on shore against their will. Many of the ladies interested themselves greatly in raising the necessary funds, which were soon obtained by the liberality of the foreign community and the hearty co-operation of the squadron in the good work. After it was once in working order it supported itself.

The races came off on the 26th, and were well attended by foreigners and Japanese, who crowded out in carriages, gin-rick-shas, and on foot. It was a gay and lively sight; a band played between the races, and many ladies were present. The course is laid out on the top of some low hills a mile or two from the town.

On the 28th of October the "Iron Duke," "Cadmus," "Frolic," "Dwarf," and "Salamis," got under weigh from Yokohama, and proceeded to Kobé in the Inland Sea, where we arrived on November the 1st, after a boisterous passage. The gales in Japan come on very suddenly and are very local; a strong wind and heavy sea is often met with off the long capes that stretch out from the land, while in the different gulfs and bays near, the weather is much finer. The wind often blows with great violence down the Kii Channel, while at the same time inside the Isumi Nada, or that part of the Inland Sea it leads into, and which is only a short distance from it, there may be very little wind at all. Many of these sudden changes are due to the high temperature of the Japan current that runs along the coast.

On the 5th the Admiral left Kobé with the squadron to go to Nagasaki, while the "Dwarf" was ordered to remain to carry out the duty of senior officer's ship in the Inland Sea. We were all sorry to part with those whom we had travelled with so far and for so long a time.

CHAPTER VIII.

KOBÉ—SHANGHAI—THE HOMES FOR SEAMEN—REBELLION AT SAGA IN JAPAN—SEARCH FOR THE CREW OF A SCHOONER THAT HAD FOUNDERED—KITE FLYING FESTIVAL.

THE autumn at Kobé is very pleasant, the temperature ranging from 47° to 60° by Farenheit's thermometer; and fresh westerly winds prevail with a bright sky. The trees assume their rich red and copper-coloured autumnal tints, which are much brighter than those in England, and make the walks about the hills most enjoyable. On one occasion I took a walk with some friends through the town of Hiogo, to visit the lighthouse at the entrance to the bay, and also the public cemetery for criminals, where the bodies of those who were too poor to pay for their funeral, and who had no friends to see that they were decently buried, were thrown together with the bodies of the criminals. The cemetery was placed at the corner of one of the very ancient burial grounds near some old temples, and consisted of a large pit about fifty feet long and ten broad. It was covered by a wooden roof, but was open at the sides. The bodies of the dead were simply thrown in, and left there to be devoured by dogs and birds, as the pit was not deep and there was nothing to keep them off. It was a most disgusting sight; but I am glad to say that the Japanese authorities have at last had it filled in with earth, and decided to bury in a more civilised manner in future.

I found the Japanese Governor of Kobé, with whom I became acquainted, a very enlightened man, and anxious for the improvement of the town and harbour. He had been trying hard to induce his government to consent to the expenditure of sufficient money to render Kobé a convenient and safe harbour by running out a pier at each end of the bay, and thus enclosing a port large enough to hold a considerable fleet of merchant ships in safety. I was shown the plan that had been made of the intended harbour. The depth of water would commence at five fathoms, which would gradually lessen towards the shore, where there would be three fathoms close in to the beach. This scheme would be of great advantage to the town, and increase the trade greatly, Kobé being so well situated with regard to the Inland Sea, and the large towns and rich country lying between it and Quioto, with which it will soon be connected by rail.

The cambers, or small harbours for boats, are only sufficient for the protection of the native junks; the foreign vessels are compelled to anchor in the bay, which is exposed in typhoons, which sometimes cause great loss of life and property.

The typhoons here generally commence with the wind from the N.-E., which drives the water out of this part of the Inland Sea (called the Isumi Nada) through the Straits of Akashi, into the Harima Nada, which is the next portion; it also drives the water out through the Kii Channel to the southward. Afterwards, when the wind gradually changes round to the S.-E. and then S.-W., the water returns with great violence through the straits, causing it to rise over the usual high water level, and add the dangers of a flood to those of the violent tempest. During a typhoon a few years ago, the water rose so high that it broke over the bund and flooded the town, the wind and waves at the same time breaking the junks on the shore, and also those foreign vessels that were not very securely anchored.

On the 4th of December, we left the anchorage at Kobé for a cruise in the Inland Sea, and to examine a shoal that had been reported. The first night we anchored in the same harbour at Sozusima, where we had previously anchored with the squadron. From thence we went to the Island of Awa-sima, and anchored in its curiously formed harbour; we carefully examined the place where the shoal had been reported, but could find no traces of it; the soundings all over agreed most accurately with those given by the last survey which was made by the captain and officers of H.M.S. "Sylvia."

A stranger would not readily make out the entrance to the harbour until quite close to it, on account of the great similarity between the hills on the island, and those on the land behind; there are also many more islands outside that make it still more puzzling. The island appeared like two hills joined together by a strip of sand. There was a village on the island, and several on the other side of the harbour, where the country was very mountainous. A few ducks and pigeons were shot by some of the officers on the island.

From this harbour we steamed across the Bingo Nada, to the anchorage off the town of Miwara which is situated on the Aogi-seto, or strait of Aogi. There is a large castle at this town, which must have formerly been a very important place, as it commands the channel which leads from the Bingo Nada to the Suwo Nada, or portion of the Inland Sea lying farther to the west. The castle was surrounded by double moats and two lines of ramparts, which were about twenty feet high and faced with stone; watch towers were built on the angles of the walls, and were in a good state of preservation. Indeed, it looked as if its owner had only lately left it, the condition was so good. The town was not large, but possessed many curiosity shops, some of which contained great quantities of armour, bows, arrows, and spears, that had formerly belonged to the castle, and been sold when the owner had retired into private life. Some of the suits were beautifully made of steel, inlaid with gold; some of them made of chain, and some of small pieces of bamboo, which they said would turn a sword cut. The helmets were fitted with curious iron masks to fit the face exactly, and which gave a most diabolical expression to the countenance, as they were made with a long aquiline nose and strongly marked features, with a sneering sinister look. There was enough common armour, spears, bows, and arrows to arm a regiment, and to be purchased at a very cheap rate.

The high road and telegraph line between Yeddo and Simonoseki, run through this town, but there did not appear to be much trade done here. A large alluvial plain extends for a long distance between the hills, and was well cultivated with rice, sugar cane, and sweet potatoes; a small river runs through the plain. The country all round is very mountainous; this part of the Inland Sea, where the narrow straits wind between the mountains and hills, and islands separate one strait from another, is considered one of the most beautiful of Japan. In the spring and autumn it certainly

JAPANESE JUNK.

deserves that character; but in the winter the hills look very bare and barren, although they are actually well cultivated. The Japanese junks with their white sails and peculiar build like the ancient Roman vessels, are a very striking feature in the scene. The crews loll about and evidently take life very easily; when the wind or tide is foul, they anchor till it becomes fair, and care little how long they are on the voyage provided they arrive safe at last. With their wooden anchor and hemp cables they are able to anchor in deep water without much inconvenience; and they are excellent sea boats, being able to ride out any ordinary gale like a duck on the water, but in typhoons great quantities of them are lost. The small fishing boats are built very sharp at the bow, and broad at the stern, they have one mast with a square sail that is placed abaft the centre of the boat which sails capitally, and beats well; the bow is high out of water, as the crew sit down in the hinder part of the boat.

From this place we weighed under sail, the tide being fair, and returned to Kobé in time for a very good theatrical entertainment given by the residents, and to which we were kindly asked. Everyone at Christmas strove to amuse themselves and their neighbours, as very little business was done in consequence of the Japanese having altered the date of their New Year to that of western nations. The holidays were kept for ten days in all their government offices, the merchants and tradesmen keeping as many as their means would allow. It is the occasion for exchanging civilities, making visits and giving presents. At the gates to the Buddhist temples the priests hang a large rope made of the last year's rice straw, and also place pieces of thick bamboo in the ground to remind Buddha to give them a good harvest of rice and plenty of bamboos; the bamboo being valuable, not only on account of the wood, but also as an article of food; the young shoot is dug up soon after it appears above the ground, it is then cut in slices and boiled, making a delicious vegetable, especially if it is served up with butter.

On the 7th of January, 1874, we left Kobé to go to Nagasaki; we experienced strong foul winds on the way which caused us to anchor occasionally behind the islands. Near the Straits of Simonoseki, the hills were covered with snow down to the base, and the N.-W. winds were piercingly cold. We passed through Spex's Strait, inside of Hirado Island, with a strong fair tide which shot us through the narrow passage very quickly. There is a town and castle at the narrowest part, and a few junks were anchored in the harbour. The Portuguese had their trading settlement at this place about A.D. 1600, and it was consequently a great stronghold for Christianity at that time.

We only remained at Nagasaki for a short time, being ordered on to Shanghai, where we were glad to meet our friends on board the " Cadmus."

There was a very respectable force of volunteers at Shanghai at this time, consisting of infantry, artillery, and a small force of cavalry called "Rangers," who were mounted on ponies, which were active and well suited for scrambling into the ditches which intersect the country. The fire brigade forms a fine strong company and were dressed in their professional dress, consisting of a red shirt and felt hat with a cock's feather.

In order to have a day's exercise and amusement, it was arranged between the officer commanding the volunteers and the captain of the "Cadmus," that a field-day and sham fight should take place between the volunteers and our blue jackets and marines who were to form a naval brigade. The plan of operations was, that the naval brigade should attack the settlement from the land side, having been landed and taken up their position beforehand; while the volunteers were to defend it. About 200 men were landed from the "Cadmus" and "Dwarf," with one field-piece and an ambulance for the wounded. As they landed about 10 A.M they carried their dinners with them in their havresacks. The officer in command, and two midshipmen who acted as aides-de-camp were mounted, and the army marched out bravely with band playing and colours flying to take up their position. In the afternoon the volunteers, who could only manage to scrape together about 100 infantry, one field-piece, and twenty Rangers, (about one third of their whole force,) marched out to meet the invaders. The attacking party advanced under the cover of some large Chinese graves, which were made of mounds of earth about ten feet high; they sent scouts to climb the trees, and to telegraph with flags the movements of the enemy. The defending forces also advanced slowly, feeling their way with the Rangers, who were occasionally rather bothered by the quantity of deep ditches. As soon as the forces came within range they commenced firing blank cartridge, and the cavalry made some gallant charges, until at last they received a volley at a short distance, which so effectually frightened the ponies that they would not face it again; they were further discomfited by receiving a charge from a small party of blue jackets, who ran after them in a comical manner, one poor pony being slightly pricked behind. Many Chinese as well as foreigners came out to see the fun; some of the former were in Gin-rick-shas, one of which was taken advantage of to afford cover for some of the sailors to fire from. The coolie who had drawn the carriage had run away in a fright, leaving a fat old Chinaman sitting in it. Telling John Chinaman to sit still, one blue jacket used his rifle on each side of the vehicle, and another from underneath, frightening the old fellow nearly out of his wits. According to what had been previously arranged the volunteers held their ground bravely for a time, but being outflanked had to give way, and were driven back to a place where some public-spirited gentleman had provided a barrel of beer; both armies ceased from their battle, fraternised, quenched their thirst with the good liquor, and marched into the settlement together after a very good day's fun.

Shanghai possesses a temperance hall for seamen and marines belonging to the vessels in port of whatever nation they may belong to. It was commenced by the clergy and residents who subscribed liberally towards it, and is now nearly self-supporting; the regular profits being greatly assisted by lectures and readings which are given occasionally in the evening by some of the gentlemen of the place, and are generally well attended as they are very amusing and the entrance fee is small. The establishment contains a reading-room and library for the seamen, who are able to get good beds there and excellent meals at a very reasonable rate; this does away with the necessity of their frequenting public-houses while on leave, where they would be charged high for indifferent food and poisoned with bad liquor. A particularly unwholesome description of spirit is sold at the low pot-houses and Chinese shops to sailors, which makes them nearly mad even after taking only a small quantity; it produces all the symptoms of poisoning, causing illness for some days, far more than is usually caused by a drunken debauch; those that indulge are usually robbed of their money as well. This spirit was sold under the name of gin, but when analyzed was found to possess little real gin in it, but to be a most noxious mixture.

Many of the missionaries, both English and American, and also the missionary ladies, devoted a portion of their time for the benefit of the seamen, by holding prayer-meetings, which they were invited to attend, at their houses in the evenings. One evening I attended at a meeting at the house of a lady who was the widow of a gentleman who had belonged to the United States consular service. The service was conducted in the drawing-room, which was conveniently fitted with folding doors to admit of the dining-room also being added when the number of people was very great, as in the present instance. Nearly 100 seamen and marines of the "Cadmus," "Dwarf," and the United States Corvette "Lackawanna" were present. The service consisted of singing, prayers and exhortations, which were given by the missionaries, some of the ladies, and also by the seamen; all of whom spoke with great earnestness, some even with eloquence; the congregation was most attentive and several of them appeared deeply moved.

We remained at Shanghai for a month, during which time we had not a single case of drunkenness or of leave-breaking by any of the ship's company; this I attributed partly to the men having a good and respectable place to go to while on leave to read and amuse themselves, and to the good influence exerted by the missionaries and those that took an interest in their welfare.

I have reason to believe that the efforts of the Christian missionaries among the Chinese will be greatly assisted by a little attention bestowed on the crews of vessels visiting the treaty ports; because the Chinese naturally value a religion according to the effect it has on the conduct of the people who profess to belong to it. When they see Christians leading godly and sober lives and regarding the sabbath, they hold respect to their faith more than when they find them regardless of all Christian duties and giving themselves up to drunkenness and immorality. Looking at the case even in its lowest and most worldly view, our country and service gains enormously by the health of the ships' companies being vastly improved by more regular and sober habits during their leave. A great cause of the large quantity of invalids that are sent home from the Chinese station being from the effects of diseases which might have been avoided by a sober life; the climate alone is sufficiently trying even for the most prudent without anything else being added to it. I have often heard it remarked by captains and commanding officers of vessels stationed at Shanghai, at Hankow, and at Tientsin where the residents on shore have interested themselves in providing places for the seamen to frequent, and the clergy have exerted themselves in their spiritual wants, that the change in the behaviour of the ships' companies has been quite evident. Although of course in many cases some of them fall back into their old habits when they arrive at places where it requires moral courage to withstand the many temptations of a seaport; yet on the whole, great progress has been made in the right direction, and the country is gradually acquiring a much steadier race of naval seamen than it possessed formerly; at the same time, the seamen retain all the zeal and daring that is required in carrying out their duty in all parts of the world and under any circumstances.

Other ports besides those I have mentioned have

also begun to turn their attention to the subject. For instance, at Amoy one of the Church of England missionaries kindly allowed the seamen to make use of a room in his house to read and to meet in, although his house was barely large enough for himself and family. At last so many came, that the residents generously decided to build or rent a small place where they could go, and I trust the scheme has been carried out. At Nagasaki a very good building was rented, and the home just got into good working order and was commencing to pay its own expenses, when it was blown down in a typhoon; at the same time great destruction was done to the rest of the houses in the town and the ships in the harbour.

Shanghai is noted for the variety and cheapness of all sorts of meat and game in the winter. Good beef, mutton, and pork; and plenty of deer, pheasant, duck, and snipe can be bought in the market, and also capital fish. The beef was about threepence-halfpenny a pound, and the pork threepence; the deer a dollar and a half or two dollars each, and the pheasants sometimes six or eight for a dollar. Those merchants that can spare the time to go away up the river in their comfortable houseboats for ten days or a fortnight, are able to shoot enough deer and pheasants, not only to supply the tables of their houses at Shanghai for some time, but also to send a large quantity to their friends at the southern ports, where game is scarce.

On the 21st of February, 1874, a telegram arrived from Nagasaki to say that a rebellion had broken out near that place, and that the rebels were marching on the town. In consequence of there being no English ship of war at Nagasaki, the "Dwarf" was ordered to go across to that place at once to protect British interests. On our arrival there on the 24th, we found that H.M. ship "Ringdove" had already come from Kobé on the same errand. A Russian corvette, a gun-boat of the United States, and a Japanese iron-clad (the old "Stonewall") were in the harbour. Arrangements had been made at a meeting of the consuls and the captains of the foreign war vessels to land 250 men from the ships to protect the foreign settlement if it should become necessary to do so for the safety of the people living on shore. The Japanese Governor had about 1000 soldiers in the town and vicinity to defend the paths over the hills.

The rebellion had broken out at a place called Saga, which is a large town about sixty miles from Nagasaki. Some noblemen and samurai had taken up arms and attacked the governor and the garrison who had taken refuge in the castle, which unfortunately had not been properly supplied with provisions for a siege, this outbreak being quite unexpected. Finding they could not take the castle by storm, the rebels managed to set fire to the towers and wood-work, after which the garrison surrendered, as many of them were killed and the rest had nothing to eat. Nearly the whole of these soldiers, including the governor, were killed most barbarously. The reason given for this rebellion was, that the governor of Nagasaki had not allowed a deputation that the people of Saga wished to send to the Mikado to present a petition, to pass through his district to embark for Yeddo.

The cause of their wanting to petition the Mikado was stated to be that the allowance of rice which had been given them by the government when the feudal system was abolished, was not sufficient for them to live on, and it was rumoured that the government intended to cease paying this allowance altogether in a few years. They were also dissatisfied that the government had not made war on the Corea, to avenge the insult lately offered to the Japanese ambassadors, when they had been sent to demand the arrears of tribute from that country. The governor had not allowed this deputation to pass, because, by Japanese law, any governor who allowed a petition to be sent from or through his district, would be liable to be disgraced for doing so.

All sorts of rumours were constantly brought into Nagasaki about the progress that the rebels were making; at one time they were reported to be only seven miles from the city. To add to the excitement, incendiaries had been arrested in Nagasaki and executed. At the first outbreak, the governor and Japanese officials got everything ready to save themselves by flight, as it was believed that he would be the first victim; but the arrival of government troops soon reassured them, and they took measures for defence instead. This rebellion appeared to have nothing to do with any enmity to foreigners; indeed the rebels had sent into Nagasaki an English doctor, who was employed by the Japanese government to attend to their hospital at Saga, in order that he might receive no injury. They also took care to send his baggage after him the next day.

On this occasion the Japanese government found the advantage of the telegraphic communication that they had established in all parts of Japan. Information of the rising was telegraphed to Yeddo before the line was cut by the rebels; the government thereupon sent troops to a town called

Fukuoka on the coast, where they were quickly landed and marched to Saga; by their promptness they defeated the rebels, and took the city before the rebellion had time to spread and become serious. Some of the leaders were taken, and afterwards tried and executed, but the authorities behaved leniently to the rest. The Japanese soldiers that were sent, were armed in the European style, and their artillery was particularly well adapted for use in this mountainous country. The guns were light, and carried along the path by coolies, for which purpose they were slung to strong bamboo poles; the carriages were taken to pieces and carried in the same manner. It took a great quantity of coolies to carry a mountain battery. The regular infantry were small wiry men and marched well; they were armed with rifles, and wore a uniform resembling the French in the cut, on account of their instructors having been principally French. The marines were a finer body of men, and dressed like the marine artillery in England; their instructor had been an officer in the English service. The militia wore the native dress.

As soon as matters became quiet, the "Ringdove" returned to her station at Kobé, and the "Dwarf" was ordered to remain at Nagasaki.

While here I took the opportunity to examine the

coal mine at Tako-sima, which is an island outside of the harbour, and about eight miles from the town. The mines were worked by the Japanese government, under the management of an English engineer who kindly showed me everything. The shaft was about 260 yards deep, and some of the galleries were driven below the sea, requiring steam pumps to be kept constantly working to prevent the salt water from accumulating and flooding the mines, as the strata is very leaky, and they have on one or two occasions driven into some old workings that had been done by the Japanese in former times. On one occasion when this took place, the old gallery they broke into was full of water and the mine was flooded, and many Japanese miners were drowned. The lower seam of coal was about nine or ten feet thick. It was a pretty good coal, but made a great deal of smoke and clinker. There were nineteen Englishmen employed in the mines; and several Japanese were studying engineering, in order that they might take charge of it themselves some day. There were many women employed, who wore a light dress, while the men wore very little indeed; all of them washed themselves constantly in the water courses leading to the pumps along the side of the gallery, and containing a plentiful supply of salt water.

On the 26th of March a meeting was held in the foreign settlement to endeavour to raise the funds to establish a sailors' home. The question whether it was to contain a canteen for the sale of beer, or be conducted on the total abstinence from intoxicating liquor principle, caused a great difference of opinion at the meeting, and threatened to shipwreck the home altogether. After much discussion it was agreed that no beer or other intoxicating drink should be sold in it, there being so many places outside where they could get any drink they wished. As soon as the motion was carried the consuls, merchants, and residents subscribed most liberally towards it, and a committee was formed to carry the work out. A building was soon hired, and fitted up with a reading-room, bowling-alley, and about eight bed-rooms; a bagatelle board was supplied, and the residents kindly sent in their newspapers for the use of the reading-room when they had finished with them; many books were also given. The charges were moderate, and a steady good man having been obtained to superintend it, with two or three Japanese servants, it soon commenced to pay for its own expenses, as there were generally several vessels of war, either English or American, in the harbour. The establishment of this place proved a great boon to the seamen, who now have plenty of leave when in harbour, and soon find the advantage of being able to land for a quiet stroll among the hills, and then to have a clean and comfortable place to get their meals and read the papers before going on board again in the evening. Unfortunately the typhoon that occurred in the autumn damaged the house so seriously that it had to be closed, but I believe only for a time, until sufficient funds could be collected to repair it.

The resident English clergyman devoted much of his time, and also a room in his house in the evening for the instruction of those seamen who wished to attend, and, as far as one could judge, his efforts were not without success. This work was undertaken by him in addition to his duties at his church and with the Japanese.

On the 11th of April a boat that had belonged to a small English schooner came into the harbour with five Japanese sailors in it. They stated that the schooner had foundered at sea in one of the late severe gales, and that the captain, who was an Englishman, and three other Europeans and eight natives had left the vessel at the same time in a larger boat. These Japanese said that soon after they left the schooner the weather had moderated, and that they had been able to land on the Meac-sima Islands, and from thence had made their way to the Kosiki Islands, which are nearer to Japan, and are inhabited. They had suffered much from want of food, but were well fed and liberally treated by their countrymen at Kosiki, where they fortunately were picked up by an English pilot boat belonging to Nagasaki, and taken by her to that place.

As the master of the schooner and his boat with the crew were still missing, the "Dwarf" put to sea to search for them. We embarked an officer belonging to the British consulate to act as interpreter, and also a Japanese official, that the governor of Nagasaki requested we should take with us to ensure that we received every assistance from the towns, villages, and places we might call at in our efforts to find the boat and people. As the schooner foundered somewhere between the Goto and Meac-sima Islands, we first called at the harbour of Tama-no-ura, which is in the former island, and enquired at all the fishing villages in the neighbourhood, but without success. The villages appeared poor, and we had a difficulty in finding any one who could read in them; there was very little cultivation, the country being rocky and mountainous. The harbour is quite secure, and has several long bays in it capable of holding a large fleet. Pheasants were numerous on the island, and fish plentiful in the harbour.

After leaving this harbour where we were detained a day or so on account of bad weather, we steamed to the Meac-sima group, which is also called the Asses Ears from the peaked appearance of the cliffs. There being no anchorage here, we sent a boat to examine the northern island, where the survivors from the schooner had first landed. On the S.E. side of this island we found a small bay with a beach of broken coral, where the boat could land, as it was fortunately quite calm; close under the cliff a small pool of fresh water and the remains of a hut were discovered, but nobody was seen at this place. The hut looked as if it had been long deserted. From this we steamed to the S.W. island of the group, which had a small bay on the south side of it. Off here we found twenty-five fathoms by sounding, although everywhere else the water was very deep indeed. We had noticed several Japanese fishing from the rocks with lines, and also from boats close to them as we came along; at the bay we found six large fishing boats hauled up on the beach between the rocks, well clear of the surf.

Our boat managed to land after some little difficulty, but could find no traces nor get any intelligence of the people we were searching for. The fishermen belonged to the Goto islands, and came here in the beginning of the year for the spring fishing, and intended to leave again before the summer when the strong southerly winds and chances of typhoons would make it dangerous to remain. They lived in temporary huts, which were made of mats, that they had brought with them and would take away again on their return home after catching and curing their fish, which consisted principally of bonito and small shark. There was a small spring of water in the cliff, and near to it were several Japanese graves with carved figures of the sailors' goddess " Matsou " placed by their comrades to take care of them on this desolate spot. The islands are small and very rugged, and have no cultivation; some of them are frequented by sea birds; boats can seldom land on them, as their position is quite exposed, and a heavy surf rolls over the coral rocks with a very moderate breeze. They are well delineated in the chart, although the reef off the east end appeared to extend farther than represented.

We then steamed to the bay in Kosiki island, where the survivors had landed after leaving Meac-sima, and from which they had been brought by the pilot boat. One of the crew that had come with us showed us the boat they had escaped in drawn up on the beach. There was a large village at the end of the bay containing a population of fishermen, and it seemed to be a thriving place, as the houses all looked neat and well built, something like those of the Loo-choo islands, and the country was well cultivated. The hills were of a moderate height, and undulating in appearance. The similarity of the houses to those in Loo-choo is accounted for by the fact that the Kosiki islands belong to the Satsuma Ken or province that conquered the Loo-choos; and Satsuma is noted for the neatness of the houses and intelligence and warlike qualities of the people. They could give us no intelligence of the missing boat that we were searching for, or the people. On my thanking the headman for the kindness and hospitality that had been shown to the portion of the crew of the British schooner that had arrived here, and requesting to be allowed to defray the expenses that the people had been put to, he said that the Japanese government had made arrangements that everything should be done to assist and relieve shipwrecked people, and that he was not allowed to be repaid for it.

Among the many advances in civilization that Japan has made, their treatment of shipwrecked people has been one of the greatest, and would do credit to any nation; the case I have just mentioned is by no means singular.

From this bay we coasted along the rest of the Kosiki islands, and then as a last chance visited the harbour of Sagitsu-no-ura, which is situated in Amekusa island, a portion of the southern part of Japan; but here also we met with no success in our inquiries. This harbour is a very good one for small vessels, but not for large ones. The country in the vicinity is very mountainous, and there are several villages scattered about the harbour and the hills. Some small rivers flow into the end of the harbour, which have gradually caused large deposits of mud to form, making it very shallow. The inhabitants have therefore reclaimed the land by raising large embankments made of faggots, clay, and mud, very thick and substantial, enclosing about 1,000 acres of land. They still continue their operations in the most persevering manner. This land will become very valuable for rice, which they had already commenced to plant. We saw great quantities of wild duck at the end of the harbour.

We now returned to Nagasaki, as we were at last compelled to believe that in consequence of the second boat having been missing so long, and the villages and fishing boats belonging to so many different places having heard nothing of it, that it must have foundered in the gale soon after the schooner did; the number in the boat, from the account of the survivors, having been more than she could take with any chance of safety in bad weather.

During our absence from Nagasaki, the cousin of the Mikado had arrived in a Japanese iron-belted corvette to enquire into the cause of the rebellion at Saga, and settle everything, having received full powers for that purpose. He was a fine looking man, and wore the naval uniform, which is very similar to the English. After finishing the business, he re-embarked in the corvette and returned to the capital. The Japanese official that had accompanied us on our late cruise wore the English dress, and was a very gentlemanly and well-mannered person. He was one of the secretaries attached to the governor, spoke English tolerably well, and ate his dinner and took to English food quite naturally. He became very popular on board, as he put up with his scanty accommodation with good humour, and only complained of sea sickness, which no one could prevent him suffering from.

For some time after the rebellion at Saga, the Japanese had been gradually concentrating large bodies of troops in the southern provinces, especially in the vicinity of Nagasaki and Kagosima, ostensibly for the purpose of preventing any further outbreak. On the 19th of April, much to the surprise of everyone, the United States Pacific mail steamer "New York," arrived to embark troops at Nagasaki, and it was rumoured that she had been chartered to land them at some place in Formosa; soon after the British steamer "Yorkshire" also arrived for the same purpose. However, the English minister at Yeddo at once decided that it would not be right to allow any vessel bearing the British flag to engage in an expedition that looked very much like a filibustering one, against a nation with whom England was at peace, and Japan had not yet declared war. A notification was therefore issued at the British Consulate, and the necessary warning given to the master of the "Yorkshire," who of course attended to it. The United States minister did the same as the British had done, although, some time afterwards, the same view was also taken by the other foreign representatives.

On the 25th of April the kite-flying festival took place at Nagasaki. Nearly all the population, men, women, and children flocked out of the city, dressed in their finest clothes, and toiled up to the top of one of the highest hills in the neighbourhood to enjoy the festival, and to make a jovial pic-nic on the hill-side. The holiday dress for the ladies and children was very neat and pretty, composed of silk of the brightest colours; the obi or thick sash, which was tied round the waist and fastened behind with the greatest care, completed the costume, and formed a most graceful *tout-ensemble*. It was curious to see the deep interest taken by all, from the grey-bearded old men to the small children, in the efforts to make their own kites fly the highest, and in the art required to manage to cut the string of any other kite that approached, by skilfully sawing it through with their own string by a few sudden jerks; and also in evading the attack of an enemy. When anyone was successful, the victim's came floundering down into the valley amidst the jeers of the conquerors. These kites were mostly made to represent hawks, or else in a square with the string placed so as to require no tail. The father of a family was generally the one to fly the kite, while the rest of the family looked on with the deepest interest, the wife making the tea and refreshing them when necessary. The greatest good humour prevailed, and they not only interchanged the civilities of the tea table with their friends, but also asked any foreigners present to join them.

CHAPTER IX.

THE JAPANESE EXPEDITION TO FORMOSA—THE ARRIVAL OF THREE CANOES AT KELUNG FROM THE PELLEW ISLANDS—JAPANESE CAMP AT LIANG-KIOU, S. FORMOSA.

THE Japanese had still continued to collect troops, stores, and guns ready for a formidable expedition; at the same time they endeavoured to keep the destination of it a profound secret by giving out that it was destined to act in case of a rebellion at home, also by spreading rumours that they wished to avenge the insult offered to their ambassadors by the Coreans. They bought two steamers to use as transports, in consequence of the foreign governments having forbidden their subjects or citizens from assisting the undertaking. A steam corvette, bearing the flag of a rear-admiral, arrived in company with a small gun-vessel to give the necessary convoy to the transports. The transports were commanded by foreigners, but the men-of-war had no foreign officers, their own being smart and able men, who afterwards proved they could take care of their own ships on a very dangerous coast, even during the typhoon season. The telegraph between Nagasaki and Yeddo broke down just before the departure of the expedition, and when it was known for certain at Nagasaki that the expedition was destined to land at a place called Liang-kiou on the S.W. part of Formosa. The foreign ministers were therefore unable to receive any certain intelligence about it till it had actually sailed, after which the line was reported to be in working order again.

On the 3rd of May the expedition, consisting of the two war-vessels already mentioned and two steam transports, steamed out of the harbour with 1,200 troops on board, and loaded up with stores and munitions of war. Other steamers were bought afterwards, and sent away as soon as the troops could be collected and embarked in them, until about 2,500 soldiers and 1,000 coolies and cultivators were landed at Liang-kiou.

The cause of the expedition was given out soon after the departure of the squadron. It was stated that a junk belonging to the Loo-choo islands, of which Japan claimed the sovereignty, had been wrecked on the S.E. coast of Formosa two or three years before, that some of the crew had been barbarously murdered by the savages, and that the rest, after suffering great hardships, had finally succeeded in making their escape to Takow, from whence they were sent home by the Chinese authorities. In consequence of China having possession of a part of Formosa, and claiming the whole of it, the Japanese stated that they had applied to the Chinese government for redress, who repudiated their responsibility for the acts of the savage tribes on the east coast, over whom they said that they had no control, and that the Chinese had further told their ambassador that if they wished for redress they had better go and punish the savages themselves. The Japanese were therefore sending this expedition to avenge the murder of the Loochooans, and as it was not possible to land a large force at the place where the junk was wrecked, on account of the heavy surf and bad anchorage, they had decided on landing on the west coast immediately opposite, and marching across the island, which is only about eight miles wide at that part.

When the Chinese found what a formidable force had been landed at Liang-kiou, they denied that the Japanese had ever applied to them, or that they had ever given them permission to land an armed force in Formosa, as they now began to fear that the Japanese meditated the conquest of the whole island. From the size of the expedition, and from the reports of the Chinese officials of the number of Japanese, who, calling themselves merchants, had been travelling over and examining every part of the country for some time previously, their fears appeared to have some good foundation. At this time the people of Japan were very unsettled in consequence of the great changes that had taken place in the country, and there was a great feeling in favour of war among nearly all classes.

To stir up the people still more, the fête days of the Japanese Empress Jingu-kozu, who had partly conquered the Corea about A.D. 300, were held with great solemnity; processions took place during the day and illuminations at night. She was canonized for these exploits and for being the mother of Hachimang, who completed the conquest and had been created their God of War, and was still worshipped as such. The priests of both the Buddhist and Sintoist temples united in doing honour to the occasion.

One evening I was asked to a Japanese dinner to meet an official of high rank that I was acquainted with. The dinner was given in a very nice native house; the guests were served with dishes on little tables about a foot high and supplied with bowls for rice, fish, and the various delicacies. We had no chairs, but had to squat on our legs or recline as we best could, which I found very inconvenient and tiring after a time, although the Japanese with their short and supple legs had no difficulty in sitting on their heels or doubling their legs under them. The tables and bowls were all made of lacquered wood, and we had to eat with chopsticks, which I found a little awkward at first, but soon got into the way of managing. The lady of the house did not sit down with the guests, but attended to see that the girls kept the dishes constantly supplied and the cups of saki full. The courses seemed endless, and some of the dishes were rather strange, especially one of raw fish, which was nevertheless very good. I found the most difficult part of the entertainment to consist in drinking the numerous toasts, without offending those who desired to drink my health, by leaving heel taps in the cup, which is quite against Japanese etiquette, it being usual to reverse the cup on each occasion to show that it is empty. The spirit is called saki, and is strong, white in colour, and made out of rice. Soon after the dinner commenced several singing girls played on the guitar and sang during the meal; everyone smoked that wished. The dinner commenced at eight, and although I managed to get away quietly at eleven o'clock, it did not actually break up till one in the morning. The singing was very monotonous and shrill, and they had very little variety in the tunes.

On the 25th of May the "Dwarf" left Nagasaki to follow the Japanese expedition; after a favourable run we called in at Kelung and coaled, and obtained all the information we could about it. The Japanese war-ships had lately called in and obtained coal, much to the disgust of the authorities, who could not prevent it being supplied to them, as they had no instructions from the Central Government on the subject, and war had not yet been declared. The Japanese, with ready assurance, entered into a contract with one of the merchants to continue to supply coal to all their transports and war-vessels that should call in and require it. Many of them took advantage of this contract, as Kelung was most conveniently situated between Japan and the scene of operations in the south.

A short time before the arrival of the "Dwarf" at Kelung, three canoes, containing twelve men belonging to the Pellew islands, had reached Kelung. They had been blown away from home while fishing, and had been sixty-four days at sea, and had travelled about 1,300 miles. A fourth canoe had been driven off with them, but had parted company a few days before the others had arrived at Kelung, and had not since been heard of. They had lived on the fish they caught, and the rain supplied them with water to drink, as their bamboo vessels for holding it were very small. They had coasted Formosa, but had not dared to land for fear of being killed by the natives; at last they were fortunately set close in to Kelung, and discovered by the Europeans at the custom-house, who had them brought in. A Russian gentleman, who was in charge of the Chinese Imperial custom-house at the port, kindly took charge of them, gave them a place to sleep in, fed and clothed them, as the climate was colder than their own. The men were smaller and darker than the savages in Formosa. When they were first picked up they were in a very emaciated condition, but by the kind treatment they received they soon recovered. On finding their way on board the ship they appeared in good spirits and were much petted by the seamen. In consequence of the great difficulty of getting these people back to their homes again, there being no communication between Kelung and the Pellew islands, they were sent to Hongkong in an English steamer, and from that place an English man-of-war eventually took them back to the Pellew islands. Their canoes were very like those at Point-de-Galle in Ceylon, being only about two feet broad, and fitted with an outrigger, which had a small neat house built on it about two feet and a half high, to give them some little shelter.

The great distance these people had travelled without landing, and the length of time that they existed at sea while drifting about with the current, show that there is nothing absurd in the theory that America may have been peopled by men and women driven away from the Asiatic coast, and drifted across in a manner similar to the voyage of these poor fellows. Indeed I have noticed that there is a great likeness in the type of feature and colour of the skin between some of the tribes in North America and also other tribes that live on the banks of the river Amazon, far in the interior of the Brazils, and also several of the Asiatic races, such as the natives of Formosa, Inos of Yesso and Gelyaks of Siberia. While in South America I had a good opportunity for examining the different tribes, as I was sent by the English government to report on the capabilities of the river Amazon for trade, when the Brazilians first opened it to foreign merchant vessels; and by the courtesy of the Brazilian President of the province of Para, Admiral Raymundo de la Mar, I was permitted to ascend the river in H.M. ship "Sharpshooter," which I commanded at that time. This was a great privilege, as the river was not open for foreign war-vessels, but the President waived the rule in my favour, on account of my mission being in the cause of science and commerce.

After calling at Tam-sui, the Pescadore islands, Taiwanfoo and Takow, where we met H.M. ships "Thalia" and "Hornet," we proceeded to Liang-kiou Bay, and anchored off the Japanese camp on June the 8th. The bay is an open roadstead, and is a safe anchorage in the N.E. monsoon, when the wind blows regularly along or off the land, but is very dangerous in the S.W. monsoon or summer time, when the winds are irregular and blow on to the shore, sending in a very heavy sea with very little warning. It is a fatal place to be caught at in a typhoon. These storms are not unfrequent, in consequence of the south end of Formosa being in the track of typhoons that are travelling towards the China coast, by way of the Bashi Channel, or of those that are travelling towards Japan along the east coast of Formosa. It was therefore needful to keep the ship prepared to steam away well clear of the land on the slightest warning of a typhoon approaching.

When the Japanese had first landed, they made their camp among the low sand ridges near the beach; the camp was made of tents, and was clean and well kept. Afterwards, when the summer advanced and the weather became too hot for living under canvas, they moved to another camp that they had made of wooden huts with double roofs of thatch, about a mile farther off and more inland. The second camp had something the appearance of a Japanese village; the floors of the huts were raised off the ground to keep them dry, and a hospital was erected, and every precaution taken for the health of the troops. The first camp was broken up when the second one was finished. There were no warships at Liang-kiou when we first arrived, but afterwards the Japanese steam corvette and gunboat, and also transports, came in occasionally, bringing stores and munitions of war, and taking away any sick people that it was necessary to send to Japan. The vessels never remained longer than they could help at anchor in the bay.

The Chinese town of Liang-kiou was situated about a mile and a half inland. The mountains commenced abruptly about two, or two and a half miles from the beach; between them and the sea the land was fairly cultivated with rice and sweet potatoes; several Chinese villages were scattered about. From this there could be no doubt that the place where the Japanese had made their camp was *bonâ fide* Chinese teritory. The savages held possession of the mountains, and were in a constant state of warfare with the Chinese settlers on the low country.

I visited the Japanese general, "Saigo" by name. He was a follower of the Prince of Satsuma, and was a fine-looking man, all the more so for being in his national dress when I saw him. Most of the troops wore a white cotton uniform, which was cut after the French fashion; they were armed with rifles. The rest, with the agriculturists, wore the national dress, and were indifferently armed. There were several field-pieces in the camp; the troops appeared to keep their weapons in good order. The Japanese hired Chinese from the neighbouring villages to assist their own people in making the huts, gardens, and also in laying out the roads in the vicinity of the camp. The troops numbered about 2,500, and the Japanese coolies about 1,000 besides.

Soon after this expedition had landed, a force had been sent inland, which had penetrated the mountains, and notwithstanding the resistance made by the warriors of the Bootan tribe, succeeded in capturing their villages and in holding the country right across the island, and from thence to the southern extremity, embracing a tract of country about nine miles square. It was the Bootan tribe who had massacred the unfortunate Loo-chooans. Several of the savages had been killed in the storming of a stockade, which had been well placed in a pass in the mountains. The Japanese loss was very small in the engagement, as they went at it with a dash and carried it quickly before the defenders had time to recover from their surprise at the sudden onset. The savage tribe was armed with matchlocks, bows and arrows, and spears; many of these were captured and sent to Japan along with a little savage girl, who had also been found in a village when her friends had fled. To prevent the Bootans giving them any further trouble, a small camp was established on the banks of a stream which ran into a bay off the eastern side of the island, where they could communicate with their vessels in fine weather. This bay was about eight miles from Liang-kiou, in a straight line, although, of course, as the road lay through the mountains, it was not an easy journey, and was exposed to the attacks of the Bootans, who still hung about the woods, and cut off any Japanese that they could, running away with the head and leaving the body to show their handiwork.

To the south of the Bootans the country was inhabited by a confederation of eighteen tribes, who acknowledged the supremacy of one chief in matters affecting the general welfare of the whole, although each tribe was governed by its own chief in all affairs which concerned itself alone. These tribes had sent a deputation to the Japanese general, soon after the expedition had landed, to offer their friendship, which of course the Japanese gladly accepted; but the eighteen tribes were not required to take any active measures against their neighbours, the Bootans. In all intercourse with the neighbouring tribes the Japanese gave forth that they had merely come to avenge the death of their countrymen, and at the same time they requested the good-will of those tribes that were not implicated in the murder, stating that the Japanese were of a kindred race to the natives who lived on the east coast and owned no allegiance to China.

While at anchor off Liang-kiou, our ship's company amused themselves by trying to catch fish with the seine near the entrance of a small river close to the camp. Many of the Japanese soldiers came down and joined in the fun; but when they had hauled the seine in and found no fish in it, they all ran away laughing, and did not come again. Very pretty red coral grows on a bank near the shore; it is formed like a honeycomb with very small cells, very curious, but I fancy of little value for manufacturing, as it is not the coral used for working up, and it is very brittle.

On the 12th of June we weighed, and worked round the south end of the island under sail, and anchored at a small bay on the east coast, where the before-mentioned Japanese camp was situated. We found the Japanese corvette at anchor here. It was near this place that the unfortunate junk was wrecked. The mountains in the vicinity come right down to the sea, with only a narrow strip of rock and sand at the end of the bay, where the Japanese had about three or four companies of soldiers encamped. A heavy surf ran on the beach, but in moderate weather a boat could land at the entrance of the small river. From this place we ran round the southern extremity again, and anchored in South Bay, which must be a capital anchorage in the N.E. monsoon, but should never be used by a sailing vessel in the S.W. monsoon, as she would have a difficulty to get out of it in bad weather. We made a survey of the bay, which is well protected from everything, except winds from the S.W., S., or S.E., and possesses very good holding ground, the bottom being of a thick sort of sand. There were several sandy beaches in different parts of the bay, and as there was no surf on them, our people were very successful with the seine, and caught some fine fish. They made a fire on the beach, cooked their suppers in the evening, and enjoyed themselves much. On the last day that they fished there, a light breeze sprung up from the S.E., which gradually sent a little swell in; and after the sun went down and they had eaten their suppers, it increased so rapidly that the party had some difficulty in getting off to the ship. Fortunately we had always taken the precaution to anchor the cutter, which was the largest boat, well outside of where the surf would break, the dingy or small boat being used to lay out the seine and take the men backwards and forwards from the cutter to the shore. While trying to get off, the small boat was capsized by a wave, and the men and net rolled over and over together with the boat. However, the men that could swim looked after those few men that could not, and soon got them out to the cutter in safety. They then swam back again and hauled the dingy up and baled her out, and after placing the net inside, managed to get her through the surf, and they all returned on board in high glee at their adventure.

All the villages near the S.W. point of Formosa were peopled by Chinese and Peppo-hoans, and owned allegiance to China. On the east side of the bay, the savage tribes held the country, and were constantly fighting with their more civilized neighbours, who have to keep their weapons by them ready for use while cultivating their fields. The natives fished principally in the evening from catamarans, using fires like those at Kelung and Sau-o-Bay. Their lights extending across the bay had a very pretty effect. In the narrative of Lord Anson's voyage, it is mentioned that while passing the south end of Formosa in October, 1742, he saw a great quantity of lights, and believed them to be made by the natives to invite his ship to approach and visit them. I expect that the fishermen at that time were merely following their trade in the same manner that they do in the present day, and hardly more anxious for a visit from strangers than they are now.

There was a very strong current running to the eastward through the Bashi Channel, which lies between the south end of Formosa and the Bashi Islands, but we found that close inshore there was a slight eddy, which was taken advantage of by junks going to the westward. There is always a nasty dangerous sea in the centre of the channel, caused by the strong current and irregular bottom.

At one of the villages that was inhabited by Peppo-hoans, they showed me a little Japanese flag, which they said had been given to them by people belonging to a Japanese gunboat, that had visited the place. On receiving it, they had been told that it was merely to prevent any small body of Japanese troops from molesting them, and to show that they were "good men," and did not belong to the savages. They appeared rather proud at having been called good men. These villagers said that they were very glad that the Japanese had come, because everything was peaceable now, although before their arrival they were constantly attacked by the savages.

After a few days we returned to Liang-kiou, where we had hardly anchored before a British subject, a native of Penang, came on board in a most distressing state, from want of proper food, and also suffering from a severe attack of fever. Of course he received every attention, and we carried him to Takow as soon as possible, and placed him in the hospital, where the poor fellow ultimately died. He said he had been employed as an interpreter by some foreigners who were employed by the Japanese, and that he had fallen ill and they had then turned him adrift.

On the 21st of June, a Chinese mandarin of high rank, accompanied by M. Giquel, who had lately held the appointment of Director of the Foo-Chow Arsenal, proceeded to Liang-kiou with three Chinese gun-vessels, to endeavour to induce the Japanese to quit the island, as they had now succeeded in effectually punishing the murderers of their countrymen. The Japanese General received them courteously, but stated that he could not leave without orders from Japan; indeed he had no transports to go in if he wished to. Before the negotiations terminated, a gale came on, driving the gunboats away, and compelling the commissioners to return by land, a very fatiguing journey. Before leaving the town of Liang-kiou, they had sent for the chiefs of the neighbouring tribes, and induced those that came to acknowledge allegiance to China, and sent them away with presents. They also issued the following Proclamation.

TRANSLATION.

Notification issued by P'an, Treasurer for the Province of Foukien, Assistant Imperial Commissioner for arranging matters in Formosa, and H-sia, Taotai of Taiwan, &c.

21 *June*, 1874.
TUNG CHIH, 13. 5. 8.

"WHEREAS the Japanese have brought an army to Formosa, to revenge themselves upon the Bootan savages for the murder of a number of Loo-chooans who were wrecked near the Bootan village; and their army has been here ever since the third month (April-May), and has not been withdrawn;

and they also wish to take vengeance upon the inhabitants of Pelam and the neighbouring villages, on the alleged ground of their having plundered a certain Japanese ship that was wrecked.

"I, the Commissioner, have received the command of the Emperor to come over to Tai-wan, and assist the Imperial Commissioner Shên in arranging the affair.

"Now, the Bootan savages who killed the Loochooans are certainly barbarous murderers; but as the place where they live is under Chinese government, if the treaty is to be observed, they of course ought to be punished by China.

"As regards Pelam and the other villages; the Japanese who were shipwrecked there last year were rescued and protected and delivered to the mandarins of Ch'ên-an-shêng (Tan-an-sing) the local chief and others, and were sent back to their country. Pelam therefore has not merely given no offence to the Japanese, but has even done them a kindness.

"If one looks at what is right and reasonable, one must suppose that the latter will not proceed to harass unoffending people.

"We, the Commissioner and Taotai are now going together by steamer to Liang-kiou to have a personal interview with the Japanese Commander, General Saigo, and reason with him. We certainly shall not suffer him to go to other villages.

"We therefore issue this notification distinctly ordering the headman of each village concerned, to give our commands to the inhabitants of the savage villages and the like, to go on quietly on their daily occupation and not to be alarmed. We, the Commissioner and Taotai, will certainly find means to protect you and keep you from harm if you are unoffending."

This proclamation was posted in several towns in the south and also in the capital Tai-wan-foo.

The Japanese at this time held not only the country to the south of Liang-kiou, but had advanced their outposts as far north as the village of Hongkong, which is about eight miles from Liang-kiou, and is in an important position on account of the mountain country coming close down to the sea, and therefore enabling the Japanese to hold the road with a small force if necessary.

I often had occasion to admire the light and easy manner in which the small detachments marched to the different outposts in the hills; they always appeared cheerful and full of fun. During the first part of their residence the camp was very healthy, but towards the end of the summer the extreme heat and monotony began to tell on them, and fever broke out.

In consequence of this attempt at negotiating having failed, the Chinese commenced to pour troops into Formosa from the mainland, and to assemble a strong naval force, consisting of a very fine and powerful steam corvette and several gun-vessels; which made the harbour of Makung in the Pescadore islands their port of refuge; and visited Tai-wan and Liang-kiou when the weather was favourable. As the summer advanced we also had to be with them a good deal at Makung, as we had instructions not to risk the dangers of a lee shore more than necessary. The captain of the corvette was a fine old Chinaman, whose good fortune commenced in consequence of his having acted as pilot to the "Bittern," an English man-of-war brig in 1854, when commanded by E. W. Vansittart in the gallant action at Shepoo, where he destroyed a large fleet of piratical junks which had done immense damage to the coasting trade in China. In the action the master of the "Bittern" had been killed, and there were eighteen others killed and wounded, as the pirates fought desperately. The Chinese government afterwards took the pilot into their service, and at this time he was in command of their finest sea-going corvette, and held the rank of a military mandarin. The Chinese possess a larger vessel, a frigate that was built at Shanghai, but for some reason was not sent to sea. I also became acquainted with the captains of several other Chinese gun-vessels and found them very intelligent and active young men, having received their education at the Naval College at Foo-Chow where they were taught by English officers. Some of them spoke English, and kept their vessels, guns and crews in good order, and handled them well.

One of them generally steamed to Liang-kiou, whenever the weather was fine, to see if more Japanese troops had arrived, and then returned immediately. As Liang-kiou was only about 110 miles from Makung and they steamed at the rate of ten or eleven knots an hour, they usually got back between the gales, although at last three of them were caught in a typhoon between Takow and Liang-kiou, in which one was driven on shore and broken up, another foundered, and the third was not heard of for so long that I do not know if she was lost or not.

A day or so before very bad weather came on, I noticed that the harbour of Makung swarmed with jelly fish floating about; and on inquiring about them from the fishermen I was informed that it was a sure sign of stormy weather.

While at Takow the "Dwarf" endeavoured to tow a British barque off the beach, where she had been driven in a typhoon. In this we were assisted by the Russian imperial gun-vessel "Gornosty," whose commander had kindly volunteered his services. Although we both tugged at her with all our strength, and hove on our cables at the same time, we did not succeed in moving her, as she had been driven too far up on the sand. When this vessel had been driven on shore, three Chinese junks had been swept out of the harbour from their moorings and broken to pieces on the bar outside.

The next day, after finding we could not save the barque, we ran down along the shore and visited the river and Chinese town of Tangkang; this town is very dirty, but has a considerable junk trade as there are nearly twelve feet of water over the bar. From thence we called at the village of Hongkong, where we found a company of Japanese soldiers, who were living very amicably with the Chinese and Peppo-hoans belonging to the place. We then ran on to Liang-kiou, where we found that a heavy sea was running into the bay, and that the wind was rapidly freshening from the W.N.W., making it unsafe to anchor there; we therefore ran on round the S.W. point, and anchored in our old berth in South Bay, which was well sheltered from this wind. The weather soon got worse, and the wind gradually backed round to the S.W., causing a heavy sea to roll into South Bay. We therefore weighed on the 8th of July, and finding that we could not steam against the wind to get into the Formosa channel again to try for some safe harbour, we had to turn back and run round to the east side of Formosa, where the wind still followed us; and we finally went on round the island and anchored at Tam-sui on the 10th.

On entering the river we noticed that all the ruins of the old forts had been carefully whitewashed, and that flags were flying on them, and Chinese soldiers were plainly visible, in the hopes of frightening any Japanese vessel that might put in. The troops were principally militia, armed with matchlocks and spears, and possessing very little discipline; the levy consisted of one man from each family.

In consequence of the ship's company having been for a long time without any good fresh meat or vegetables, they were beginning to suffer from boils and ulcers, although the allowance of lime-juice had been doubled and every precaution taken by the doctor. At Tam-sui we managed to get some good fresh meat, and the men were sent to gather watercresses at a stream about a mile from the town. These cresses were eaten fresh and also boiled like spinach, and proved an excellent antiscorbutic medicine, the good effect being visible in a few days.

While at Tam-sui we heard a most curious story of the proceedings of four Japanese who had come there in the month of May, and after remaining for a short time had gone on to Kelung, where they chartered a small junk and went to Sau-o-Bay, on the east coast. From this place they hired a boat, and proceeded to the southward until they came to a small Chinese stockaded village, which was situated in the savage territory about four miles north of Chock-a-day, which is a village belonging to the savages, and situated on a small river or stream. They proceeded to Chock-a-day by land, and by making presents to the chiefs obtained permission to remain. They then settled themselves in a hut which they hired, and hoisted a Japanese flag on a hill near the sea.

Fever was very prevalent at this place, being caused by the high and steep mountains, which are overgrown with dense vegetation, and close in the valleys so as to prevent any good circulation of air, and also from the extreme dampness of the climate. The Japanese were at last seized with fever, and then after some difficulty managed to induce the savages to assist them to return to Sau-o-Bay, from whence they easily got to Kelung, where two of them embarked in the Japanese corvette that happened to be in the harbour at the time, and the other two found their way to the Japanese camp at Liang-kiou. They had left a sealed box in charge of the savages, and had told them that they would return as soon as they were recovered, and that they would bring them more presents in gratitude for the kind treatment that they had experienced. Instead of doing this, these Japanese complained to the Chinese government that they had been robbed of 1,000 dollars and ill-treated by the tribe that they had lived with.

On receiving this complaint the Chinese sent a gun-boat with a mandarin and a gentleman who was employed in their foreign customs service to enquire about the truth of the statement. After much trouble they landed at the small Chinese village where the Japanese had landed; their boat was capsized in the surf in doing so, though fortunately no one was drowned. From thence they made their way to Chock-a-day, and after making presents of pigs and cloth to the savages, obtained the sealed box and a few other articles that had been left by the Japanese. The mandarin then took care to inform them that the Japanese had come for no good purpose, and that their countrymen wished to conquer the land, but that China would protect them, and they need have no fear. The mandarin then returned to Sau-o-Bay and landed. A larger gun-boat was in the bay on their return, and was anchored in the outer part while the little one got behind the reef in a tolerably sheltered place. A typhoon came on, and the small one managed to ride it out at anchor, but the large one put to sea and was dismasted and lost all her boats: however, she eventually got to Foo-chow in safety. The sealed box and other property of the Japanese adventurers were sent to Tai-wan-foo, and from there to the Japanese consul at Amoy, with an intimation that they had no business to land at any place that was not a treaty port.

I may as well here mention that, although I do not profess to form an opinion as to the course taken by the Japanese in avenging the death of their countrymen, whether they were right or wrong in landing such a large force in Chinese territory, the effect has been very beneficial to all nations that possess vessels trading in these seas, as it has caused the Chinese to send gun-boats and officials to several savage villages on the coast, and to endeavour to induce the chiefs to be kind to any shipwrecked people that should fall into their power in future. The Japanese quite ignored the old excuse of the Chinese that they had no control over those tribes, and therefore could not be responsible for their acts.

CHAPTER X.

NAGASAKI—EFFECTS OF TYPHOON, AUGUST 20TH, 1874—SHANGHAI—CHING-KIANG—NANKING—NINGPO—HONGKONG—RELIEVED BY THE NEW SHIPS COMPANY, NOVEMBER 30TH, 1874.

ON our return to Takow we found that H.M. ship "Modeste" had arrived from Hongkong, and had brought orders for us to proceed to Nagasaki, for which place we accordingly started, and arrived on the 25th of August, after a very pleasant passage under sail.

On entering the harbour, we were much surprised to see that many of the finest trees had been violently uprooted, that a great number of houses were in ruins, that several steamers and ships had been driven on the rocks; the masts of a Japanese ironclad ("Stonewall") and of several junks were showing above the water, and there were wreckage and débris all about the beach in every direction. This havock was caused by the terrible typhoon that had taken place four days previously. The governor's European-built house had been blown down like a pack of cards; the British consulate was not habitable, although the flagstaff appeared the only one that had weathered the storm, the topmast having been sagaciously housed before the hurricane came on. The bamboos and trees that had not been uprooted were quite brown, as if they had been scorched with fire. Heavy rain had succeeded the typhoon, which made it still more miserable for the poor people, as they were unable to repair their houses, but sat shivering under the ruins till the rain ceased. However, after the rain cleared off, the Japanese soon recovered their spirits and set about repairing their houses and junks.

The foreign steamers were soon got off again, but the loss of lives from the junks that foundered was very heavy. After much difficulty the ironclad was raised by being pumped out with two large centrifugal steam pumps that an English shipbuilding firm fortunately possessed.

This typhoon came across from the S.E. like a whirlwind, and it is calculated to have had a diameter of about fifty miles; the track over the south of Japan being only too clearly marked by the damage done to houses, trees and fields; many of the latter had the crop washed off by the heavy rain after the storm.

On the 13th of September the "Iron Duke" arrived from her northern cruise, and on the 15th the "Dwarf" was sent to Shanghai. While at

Shanghai we lost one of our men, a marine, who was returning from leave of absence on shore, and unfortunately slipped off the jetty into the river in the dark. He was sucked under by the strong current and drowned. This river is always considered fatal to anyone falling into it, on account of the strong tides and eddies.

We found the Chinese busily employed in repairing the fortifications at Wusung, collecting troops in the neighbourhood, and then forwarding them on to Formosa, and making every preparation as if war was imminent. At the same time negotiations were being carried on with the usual Eastern delay, which gave ample time to the Chinese to collect their forces and send them across to Formosa. The Japanese were also mustering their troops in the south of Japan, and had several transports ready, and the people appeared eager to try their new navy and army against that of the Chinese.

When it had been known at Shanghai, that the Japanese ironclad had foundered in the typhoon, there was great rejoicing among the Chinese, as they feared the old "Stonewall" much, having no ironclad of their own; but when they heard she had been raised again, they were proportionably dejected.

On October the 12th the "Dwarf" was ordered to visit Ching-kiang, and other places on the river Yang-tze-kiang as far as the city of Nanking. On our way up we noticed that the Chinese were building forts and collecting troops at the narrow parts of the river, namely, Kiang-yin and Silver Island, evidently with the intention of giving any Japanese invaders a warm reception. Ching-kiang is a large walled town, and is a very dirty one. It has a considerable trade, as its situation is near one of the entrances to the Grand Canal. The country all round is very fertile, and the large cultivated plains are intersected by canals in every direction, which are crowded with boats of all sorts, sizes, and descriptions, bringing the produce into the towns on the river for sale and to be exported in larger vessels. From Ching-kiang towards Nanking, the country still bears evident signs of its former occupation by the rebels, although more than ten years have passed since the Tae-pings were in possession. It is painful to see the country in many places lying waste, and the large quantity of ruins of towns and villages that are overgrown with grass and bushes, and now are a shelter for deer and pheasants instead of their proper inhabitants. The Grand Canal also is nearly choked up in many places; deer and game have increased so much near its bank, that some of the best shooting in China is obtained in the neighbourhood.

About ten miles above Ching-kiang, there is a large salt depôt, which supplies the five provinces of Hunan, Hupeh, Kiangse, Anhuei and Kiangsu. The salt is brought from the districts of Tai-chow and Tung-chow, where it is collected in salt pans. The traffic is so great, that from 1,000 to 2,000 junks and cargo boats are always at this place, to load and unload their cargoes. The management of the depôt is under a Commissioner of Salt Gabelle, who is a mandarin of high rank, and has two others to assist him, the duty on salt being a source of very profitable revenue for the government. The junks are moored in tiers of ten or fourteen abreast of each other, and close to the north bank of the river opposite Deer Island. Some of the junks that come from the interior were very strange, being high and pointed at both ends, and very low in the water at the middle. On gala days they have their bright coloured flags flying, gongs beating, and the small boats dart about everywhere making a very busy and cheerful scene, as the junks are mostly clean and varnished.

At Nanking we saw the Chinese erecting new batteries for heavy guns to command the anchorage and the entrance to the creek leading to the arsenal.

They had also a camp of soldiers here, some of whom were armed with muzzle-loading rifles, others with swords, spears, or matchlocks.

The arsenal is situated on a creek that runs beneath the city walls. It is about seven miles from the entrance, and steam launches can ascend the whole way to it. When I visited it, Dr. MacCartney was the superintendent, and managed to make the Chinese workmen do everything in the place without the assistance of any other European. They were busily employed in making torpedoes, which were to contain 1,000 pounds of powder. They were fitted with a very ingenious contrivance to cause the ignition of the whole of this large charge at once, and by so doing to obtain the greatest possible effect from the explosion. These torpedoes were fitted to be fired either by electricity or concussion, and if handled by people who could understand and manage them, would effectually prevent vessels ascending the Yang-tze-Kiang. They were also busy about making Hale's rockets; but Dr. MacCartney informed me that the Chinese preferred Congreve rockets, in consequence of their finding that they possessed a greater range and lower trajectory. Gatlin guns, rifled cannon up to twenty-pounders, and smooth-bore guns up to ten inches, were being made in the arsenal. A Chinese official and a small guard of soldiers were attached for the protection of the establishment.

Close to the arsenal were the remains of the celebrated porcelain pagoda, which is now merely a heap of rubbish, of brick, tile, and porcelain, with a great iron basin on the top of it, which originally crowned the edifice, and is said to weigh twelve tons. This pagoda was destroyed by the Tae-ping rebels when they held the city of Nanking, on account of it being outside the walls and close enough to overlook them; they were afraid of it being taken advantage of by the enemy, and therefore placed some gunpowder inside the base and blew it up. The Chinese account of the pagoda is as follows:—

"THE PORCELAIN TOWER AT NANKING.

"A pagoda stood there from time immemorial, but the first mention thereof is in the annals for A.D. 241. The great porcelain pagoda was built by the Emperor Yung-So. It was begun A.D. 1413 and finished 1432. It had nine stories, and was $329\frac{1}{4}$ Chinese feet high. At the top was an iron basin containing five pearls, supposed to have magical powers, one picul of tea, 1,000 ounces of silver, a picul of brimstone, two bales of yellow satin, and sundry prayers to the various personifications of Buddha. The pagoda and buildings cost altogether 2,485,484 taels, or about £800,000. It was destroyed by the Taepings in 1853. Its name in Chinese was Pao^{ns} Ên Tá, or Pagoda of Gratitude, it having been built by the Emperor in memory of his mother."

I measured the walls of the city, and found them to be 125 feet thick at some places, and the height varied from fifty to eighty feet, according to the nature of the ground. They were about twenty miles in circumference. This will give some idea of the grandeur of Nanking in the Ming dynasty, when the emperors held their court here. The inhabited part is now very small, the rest of the ground inside the walls consisting of fields and wilderness, which afford good cover for pheasants; the shooting both inside and outside of the walls being very good. The officers made the best bags on the north bank of the Yang-tse, about nine miles from the anchorage, where they found plenty of deer and pheasants. The tombs of the Ming Emperors are outside the walls, and consist of a large mound with two avenues leading to it, one of figures of warriors carved in stone and another of animals. The figures of the men are eight in number and eleven feet high, and those of the animals are twenty in number and fourteen feet high. The temples in the city and the Tartar quarter, which formed a fortress in itself, are also worth seeing; the buildings in the latter, where the court was held, must have been very grand.

A great part of the trade on the Yang-tze-kiang is done by large and powerful steamers, which ascend as far as Hankow, and call at the different towns that are opened for trade on the way.

We returned to Shanghai on November 2nd. On the following night a seaman of the U.S. frigate "Hartford" fell into the river; fortunately one of our petty officers happened to come down the jetty at the same time and saw the poor fellow fall. He immediately jumped in after him and managed to get him into a boat and then took him off to his ship. For saving this man's life he received the thanks of the United States captain, which were conveyed officially through the Commander-in-Chief. He had already obtained the Humane Society's medal for a similar act on a former occasion.

After long negotiations the quarrel between Japan and China was at last settled; China agreed to pay to Japan 100,000 taels for the benefit of the families of the Loo-chooans that had been murdered, and a further sum of 400,000 taels for the expenses the Japanese had been put to in making roads and improvements in the south of Formosa. A tael is a little less than six shillings. Of course this sum did not represent more than a very small portion of the expense Japan had incurred in carrying out this expedition and preparing for war. The Japanese agreed to leave the island as soon as the N.E. monsoon set in, which would be about December; it would have been dangerous for them to attempt to embark before the weather had become quite settled. On their return home they were received with great rejoicings, in consequence of the honour of Japan having been satisfied in the punishment of the savage tribes, and also by the fact of the Chinese having acknowledged their responsibility by paying an indemnity for the outrage.

At a place called Xic-a-way, which is about five miles and a half from the foreign settlement, there is a large mission school, which is under the charge of Roman Catholic priests. It contains a school for 130 Chinese boys belonging to rich families who can afford to pay for their education. These have large and airy studies and good sleeping rooms allotted to them, and receive a thorough education from the priests. The college also contains another school for poor orphan boys, who are taught different trades, such as carpentering, tailoring, shoemaking, painting, &c., according to what they are best suited; so that when they leave the school they may be able to earn their own livelihood. There were about 110 belonging to the boys' orphanage, and the same to the girls'. The girls' orphanage is conducted by Sisters of the Society. The establishment contains a chapel, and also an observatory, which is supplied with a good telescope and many valuable astronomical instruments. There were eight priests residing in it, who are sometimes changed with those that require to come to the mission for their health after living among the Chinese in dirty houses and towns in other parts of the country. I was informed that the establishment was self-supporting, the wants of the priests being very small. They all wore the Chinese dress.

While at Shanghai we heard that our relief had at last arrived at Hongkong, a new ship's company having been sent out in H.M. ship "Victor Emmanuel." On the 16th of November we therefore got under way and bid farewell to Shanghai and started on our voyage to the south.

We called in at the city of Ningpo on our way, of which I was very glad, never having been there before. I was much disappointed in the appearance of the town as there were not many foreign residents; and those that were here lived in houses that are scattered about at some distance from each other, and separated by dirty Chinese streets. The city is surrounded by a wall and has one good street in it with some fine shops; but the rest of the streets were small and dirty and many of them in ruins.

Instead of burying the dead under ground, the coffins were placed among the ruins and left to rot by the action of the elements. This disagreeable custom gave a very dismal appearance to the place, and was particularly offensive to the nose and caused much fever.

The military command of the city was held by an Englishman who bore the rank and title of Colonel, and was formerly an officer in Gordon's "Ever Victorious Army," the remains of which force were stationed at Ningpo; they had dwindled down to barely 300 men, but these are well armed and drilled.

After remaining at Ningpo a few days we proceeded to Amoy, where I had the opportunity of saying good-bye to many old friends who had always shown great kindness and hospitality to the little ship when stationed here.

From Amoy we proceeded to Hongkong, and on

the 30th of November, 1874, the ship's company that had served their time were sent on board the commodore's ship, the "Princess Charlotte;" and the newly-arrived one joined from the "Victor Emmanuel." Thus ended a very pleasant commission of three years and eight months on board of H.M. ship "Dwarf!"

THE END.

www.ingramcontent.com/pod-product-compliance
Lightning Source LLC
Chambersburg PA
CBHW022105230426
43672CB00008B/1287